VON KLEIST
- FROM HUSSAR TO PANZER MARSHAL -

LANCER
MILITARIA
HOUSTON
K
TEXAS

VON KLEIST

- FROM HUSSAR TO PANZER MARSHAL -

CLYDE R. DAVIS

LANCER MILITARIA
Houston, Texas

CONTENTS

INTRODUCTION

Rommel! Guderian! Von Rundstedt! Halder! Von Manstein! Kesselring!These are names well known and often spoken among those interested in the Second World War and German military history. Yet, among the most successful and competent commanding generals of the German Wehrmacht was another officer whose name and achievements on the battlefield have somehow escaped the limelight accorded his contemporaries. That man was Generalfeldmarschall Ewald von Kleist.

Generalfeldmarschall von Kleist could almost be considered the "forgotten Field Marshal" of World War II. This is especially the case insofar as postwar American and English historical literature are concerned. Although much detailed information is currently available regarding the campaigns in which he participated and the forces which he led, virtually nothing is now in print in the English language concerning the man himself. Even in postwar German literature very little is now available to the historian and historical student interested in von Kleist. Only two current German publications concern themselves with his life — a ten-page biography by General der Panzertruppe a.D. Walther K. Nehring appearing in the 1974 edition of the *Deutsches Soldatenjahrbuch* (Schild-Verlag), and a twelve-page chapter in the book *Die Deutschen Generalfeldmarschälle 1935-1945* by Otto E. Moll (Erich Pabel Verlag). These two texts are of course in the German language, and their availability and usefulness to American historians is thereby limited.

The relative obscurity of Ewald von Kleist in the literature is puzzling. Much ado has been made in numerous publications concerning the career and achievements of Generaloberst Heinz Guderian, yet Guderian was von Kleist's subordinate in the brilliant German armored thrust through France in 1940 and (despite the high favor he found with Hitler) never received the coveted Field Marshal's baton. Perhaps at least a partial explanation of von Kleist's secondary place in historical print lies in the fact that — unlike Guderian and Rommel — he did not seek publicity and self-aggrandizement. Under the command of Ewald von Kleist, First Panzer Army spearheaded the drive of Army Group A to within 75 miles of the Caspian Sea. This was the deepest penetration of any German force into Russia. Von Kleist later received his promotion to Field Marshal for his exemplary tactics in conducting the withdrawal of Army Group A from the Caucasus — a remarkable honor considering Adolf Hitler's preoccupation with offense and loathing of retreat. Had GFM von Kleist commanded forces against the Western Allies rather than against the Russians during the period 1941-1944, it can safely be assumed that he would today occupy a far greater prominence in the literature of military history.

The objectives of this book are twofold and simple. The first of these is to provide the reader with an overview of the life and career of Ewald von Kleist. Although not an in-depth biography, it is hoped that students of the Second World War will thus be "properly introduced" to a highly competent, patriotic officer who has too long been unjustly overshadowed by his contemporaries. No attempt whatever has been made to write a history of the actual campaigns in which von Kleist participated, as that is far beyond the scope and intent of this volume. Such information is readily available to interested researchers in the current literature, and a number of the better sources are cited in the bibliography to aid those wishing to make an in-depth study of battlefield events.

The second aim of this book is to provide — both to the historian and to the militaria collector — a photographic documentation of the career of Generalfeldmarschall von Kleist and of the achievements of the troops under his command. If written data concerning von Kleist is scarce, published photographs of him are so few as to be truly quite rare. In those few books (both American and German) which have bothered to picture Ewald von Kleist, the photographs have generally been repetitive and of poor quality. The only notable exception has been the previously mentioned article by General Walther Nehring, which does contain several excellent photos. Even considering that exception, probably fewer than fifteen different photographs of von Kleist have appeared in postwar publications, and in most cases the same tired old stock "press photos" have been used over and over again ad infinitum. If it accomplishes nothing else, this volume will give both the man and his troops the photographic immortality they deserve.

Special mention is justified regarding the sources of the photographs which appear in this work. The vast majority of these photos were the personal collection of GFM Ewald von Kleist himself, and most of those are pictures taken by German Army war photographers who accompanied von Kleist in the field during the period 1941-1943. This collection of photographs was among a number of items belonging to the Field Marshal which were obtained in June 1945 near Bad Kissingen, Germany by Mr. Robert G. Mauermann. At the time of their acquisition, Mr. Mauermann was a First Lieutenant in the United States Army and was serving as Operations Officer for the 609th CIC Detachment. GFM von Kleist had been captured by American forces in April 1945, and thereafter his family had moved to the estate of Schloss Aschach near Bad Kissingen. Upon receiving information of the von Kleist family's presence in the area, Lt. Mauermann and another officer of his unit drove to the estate to search for documents and data of possible intelligence interest. The photographs were found packed for storage in a trunk, together with numerous other items belonging to the Field Marshal (including various documents and letters, one of von Kleist's uniform tunics, and his personal firearms). GFM von Kleist's personal diaries and disc recordings of his speeches were turned over to the Army by Lt. Mauermann for intelligence evaluation. The photographs, uniform, guns, and various documents of no intelligence significance were retained by Mauermann as war souvenirs and were shipped back to his family in Texas for safekeeping until his return to the United States. The majority of the von Kleist materials were subsequently obtained from Mr. Mauermann by the author in 1974.

The von Kleist photo collection consists of approximately 570 individual photographs, including over 230 picturing von Kleist himself. The remainder of the photos depict the forces under his command and the territory in which those forces operated. Because of practical space limitations it has not been possible to reproduce all of the collection here. However, every effort has been made to select and print the most significant and most representative pictures from the collection. It is believed that those selected best depict the career of GFM von Kleist and the achievements of his troops. With very few exceptions, these photographs have never before been published. Of necessity, the majority of the pictures concern the Russian Front during the period 1941-1943, since the collection primarily concerns that time. To complement the von Kleist collection itself and to fill in major gaps, a number of photographs from other sources (again essentially all never before published) have been included. Many of these have been graciously provided by living members of the von Kleist family. These additional photos provide continuity and greatly enhance the basic objective of documenting the life of Ewald von Kleist. Each photograph obtained from another source has been credited to its source, and all photographs showing no accreditation are from the personal collection of the Field Marshal himself.

ACKNOWLEDGEMENTS

The person most responsible for making this book possible is the man who plays the "title role" — Field Marshal Ewald von Kleist himself. His accumulation of the many photographs which are the heart of this volume has served to preserve a unique documentation of not only his personal career but also of one of the greatest military operations of all time — the German thrust through southern Russia. I believe sincerely that, were he alive today, GFM von Kleist would heartily approve of their publication after all these years — not from any desire for personal fame (which he never sought), but rather for the memory of the countless soldiers under his command who served their country to the best of their abilities and who ultimately sacrificed so much for their doomed efforts.

Mr. Robert G. Mauermann has played an obviously key roll in making this volume a reality. As an experienced intelligence officer, he was quick to recognize the historical significance of the photographs and documents which came into his hands at war's end. Most importantly, Mr. Mauermann took great care to preserve and safeguard this material over the many years which have subsequently passed. In other hands the von Kleist collection could easily have met a more common and ignominious fate by being destroyed, turned into children's playthings, or scattered to the four winds. Instead, the collection was kept intact, and it remains intact today.

During the course of my efforts to learn more of Ewald von Kleist, help was found from an unexpected but invaluable source. Frau Christa von Kleist, daughter-in-law of Generalfeldmarschall von Kleist and widow of his younger son, not only provided me with a number of exceptional photographs which filled in many of the gaps that otherwise would have plagued this book (especially from the early days of his career); she also made a special trip at her own expense to Houston, Texas — going many hundreds of miles out of her way during a brief vacation visit to this country — in order to see the von Kleist collection and to bring the additional photos. During her visit, this very gracious lady freely discussed personal details of the lives of the Field Marshal and his family, and willingly submitted to my almost endless questions. There is no way in which I can adequately express my gratitude to Frau von Kleist, but I sincerely hope that this book makes that gratitude clear to her in some small way.

In addition to Christa von Kleist, another member of the von Kleist family also stepped forward and gave needed data. Brigadegeneral a.D. Karl-Wilhelm von Kleist provided me with a most useful "family tree" of the Field Marshal's branch of the family, and with identifications of several of the von Kleist photographs. General von Kleist was a Panzer officer in Poland, France, and Russia, and a Major in the German Army General Staff from late 1944 until the end of the Second World War. He participated in the building of the Bundeswehr (the West German Army) and served as a field officer, as a General Staff officer, and in the Ministry of Defense. He retired from the military in 1969 as a Brigadier General.

General der Panzertruppe a.D. Walther K. Nehring, holder of the Knight's Cross of the Iron Cross with Swords and Oakleaves, deserves a very special thanks. His excellent biographical article entitled *Generalfeldmarschall Ewald von Kleist*, which appeared in the 1974 *Deutsches Soldatenjahrbuch* (Schild-Verlag), was a source of much of the information in the text of this book. From the beginning General Nehring has lent strong encouragement to me in my desire to publish the von Kleist photograph collection, and he graciously gave his permission for the use of numerous quotes from his own writings. He is a historian in his own right, having produced numerous writings on World War II (including many articles in the *Deutsches Soldatenjahrbuch*, and his own book on the history of the German Panzer forces). His expertise in such matters is clear, General Nehring himself having served as Commanding General of the Afrikakorps and as the last Commanding General of First Panzer Army (von Kleist's own command during the heyday of the Russian campaign).

Other individuals have also generously contributed photographs or other forms of support during my research. Likewise, various official government agencies have provided valuable documentation and data. Peter G. Bilheimer and Timothy F. Knight, long-time collectors and good friends, have provided photographs and encouragement. Robert Sevier and Charles Scaglione generously allowed me to borrow and photograph unique documents that formerly belonged to Generalfeldmarschall von Kleist, during the early days of my research. John R. Angolia provided from his personal collection the poignant "mug shot" photograph of Ewald von Kleist taken in an Allied prison camp. On the official side, Dr. Giessler of the Bundesarchiv (Militärarchiv) in Freiburg, W. Germany, has provided photocopies of various von Kleist documents from the Bundesarchiv collection. The U. S. National Archives has provided additional von Kleist photographs. The U. S. Army has provided the interesting photograph of the Field Marshal after his "capture" from retirement by American troops. David Burris of Port Arthur, Texas has been of much assistance by translating many source documents from the German. All of these sources and contributions have added to the continuity and completeness of this work.

Lastly — but far from least — I owe personal thanks to Donald Willis of Houston, Texas. Being neither a collector nor historian, and thus acting only out of friendship, his continual prodding and gentle harassment over the past two years have played no small part in getting me off dead center and into an active commitment to the completion of this project.

C. R. Davis
Houston, Texas
December 1979

PAUL LUDWIG EWALD VON KLEIST (seen here standing on the steps of the von Kleist family estate at **Weidebrück über Breslau, Silesia after the fall of France, 1940**)

EWALD VON KLEIST — THE MAN AND THE COMMANDER

Paul Ludwig Ewald von Kleist was born on August 8, 1881 in Braunfels an der Lahn. His father was Dr. phil. (Doctor of Philosophy) Christoph Albrecht August Hugo von Kleist, a professor and assistant master of a private secondary school, and his mother was Elisabeth von Kleist (nee Gley). Although thus not born in a military household, the future Generalfeldmarschall sprang from one of the oldest and best-known military families in Prussian-German history. The von Kleist family produced some thirty-four Generals, three Field Marshals, and thirty-one holders of the highest Prussian decoration for bravery and battlefield achievement (the Orden Pour le Merite, or "Blue Max").[1] In addition to military leaders, the von Kleist family also included famous intellectual and artistic figures — among them an earlier Ewald von Kleist (a renowned poet who died a soldier's death from battlefield wounds in 1759), and Heinrich von Kleist (mathematician, philosopher, and writer, 1777-1811).[2]

True to the tradition of his family, Ewald von Kleist chose a military career. After completing his basic schooling and passing his final examination in March 1900, he joined the Royal Prussian Field Artillery Regiment No. 3 (Kgl. Preussische Feldartillerie-Regiment Generalfeldzeugmeister Nr. 3) in Brandenburg as a Cadet (Fahnenjunker).[3] Otto E. Moll (in *Die Deutschen Generalfeldmarschälle 1935-1945*) cites 1899 as the beginning year of von Kleist's military service, but other sources and original documentation prove this to be incorrect. By authority of a commission dated October 18, 1900, he was subsequently upgraded to the grade of Fähnrich (Ensign, or Aspirant — an officer candidate rank with no English or American equivalent).[4] Upon completion of the training necessary to become a full-fledged officer, he was commissioned as a Leutnant (Second Lieutenant) of Field Artillery on August 18, 1901; as was a common German practice, his promotion was made rectroactively effective as of August 19, 1900 for purposes of senority.[5] In 1906 he became an Abteilungsadjutant (Battalion Adjutant) — noted military author General Walther Nehring gives the date as 1904 — and a year later was appointed as Regimentsadjutant (Regimental Adjutant) of Feldartillerie-Regiment Nr. 3.[6] According to at least one source, von Kleist was attached to the Reitschule (Cavalry School) at Hannover during the period 1908-1909.[7] On January 27, 1910, he was promoted once again to the rank of Oberleutnant (First Lieutenant); the original promotion document reflects that his unit at that time was still Feldartillerie-Regiment Nr. 3.[8] After completing the required examinations with high scores, the young Oberleutnant was posted to the Kriegsakademie (War Academy) at Berlin on October 1, 1910.[9] A few days later — on October 18, 1910 — he married Gisela Wachtel at Hannover. A devoted couple, the marriage of Ewald and Gisela von Kleist would endure for the remainder of their lifetimes.

Von Kleist remained at the Kriegsakademie for three years, from 1910 to 1912. On April 22, 1912, he was transferred to the 14th Hussar Regiment (Husaren-Regiment 14) at Kassel. However, he retained his posting to the Kriegsakademie until completion of the full course of instruction.[10] On March 22, 1914, he was reassigned to the staff of the 1st Prince's Own Hussar Regiment (1. Leibhusaren-Regiment Nr. 1) at Danzig, previously commanded by the German Crown Prince Wilhelm.[11] Nehring reports the date of this assignment to have been May 20, 1914. At the time of this posting, or shortly thereafter, von Kleist was promoted to the rank of Rittmeister (Cavalry Captain). As the First World War began, he went into action with his regiment against the Russians, who had launched an offensive into East Prussia. Serving as a Cavalry Squadron Commander (Eskadronchef), he took part in the great battle of Tannenberg in August 1914.[12] This battle routed the invading Russian forces and led to their expulsion from East Prussia. As the war progressed in the East against Russia, Rittmeister von Kleist held various General Staff posts. In 1916 he was on the staff of the 17th Army Corps (XVII. Armeekorps), according to Moll; General Nehring states that von Kleist was Ia (Chief of Staff) of the 7th Corps (VII. Korps). His final wartime posting came in 1917 when he was appointed Chief of Staff (I. Generalstabs-Offizier) of the Garde-Kavallerie-Division (Guard Cavalry Division); following the German-Russian peace treaty in March 1918, the division was transferred to France — where it saw action near Reims, in the Champagne region, and along the Maas River before the war came to an end.[13]

Following the end of the First World War in November 1918, and the collapse of the German monarchy, Rittmeister Ewald von Kleist served briefly in one of the many Freikorps ("voluntary corps") units of former German soldiers which arose throughout the country to combat leftist uprisings and revolutionary factions causing turmoil after the Kaiser's abdication. By this time he was already a father, his first son — Johannes Jürgen Christoph Ewald von Kleist — having been born in Hannover on July 7, 1917 as the war still raged. In the autumn of 1919 the new Reichswehr (Armed Forces) of the Weimar Republic came into official being, under severe limitations imposed on Germany by the Treaty of Versailles.[14] Von Kleist quickly returned to active military duty with the new German Army (Reichsheer). Available details regarding his early Reichsheer service are vague at best. According to information provided to the author by the von Kleist family, he served during 1919-1920 as Chief of Staff of the "Division Münster" (not further identified) and on October 1, 1920 he was serving with the Reiter-Regiment 13 (13th Cavalry Regiment). Both Moll and Nehring state that he served on the staff of the "Infanterieführers 6" (literally "Infantry Leaders 6", not further identified); Moll cites his rank at this time as Hauptmann (Captain), and Nehring dates this service in 1921. From this point on, the facts are fortunately much clearer.

On March 22, 1921, Gisela von Kleist gave birth to the couple's second and last child — another son, Hugo Edmund Christoph Heinrich von Kleist. Heinrich, like his older brother before him, was born at Hannover. Since the peacetime situation would have given little reason for an active duty army officer to reside in a state of separation from his family, it is presumed that Ewald von Kleist was residing at this time in Hannover with his wife and sons, and that his duty post was in or near that city. It is definitely known that he resided there for the following five year period, as he was assigned from 1922 through 1926 as an Instructor of Tactics at the Kavallerieschule (Cavalry School) in Hannover. On February 1, 1922, he was promoted to the rank of Major — with a date of rank retroactive to July 1, 1921 for senority purposes. According to at least one source, Major von Kleist became Kommandeur (Commander) of the Kavallerieschule Hannover in 1924.[15] Unquestionably he received a further promotion to Oberstleutant on December 1, 1926. Since a "gap" exists in his known assignment history for the year 1927, and since both Nehring and Moll state that he served as Instructor of Tactics (Taktiklehrer) at the Cavalry School through 1926 — without mentioning any duty as actual Commander of the School — it is entirely possible that he assumed the duties of "Kommandeur'' upon his promotion to Oberstleutnant and held that post until leaving the school.

From the Kavallerieschule Hannover, Oberstleutnant von Kleist was transferred to the post of Chief of Staff (Chef des Stabes) of the 2nd Cavalry Division (2. Kavallerie-Division) in Breslau, Silesia. Moll dates this reassignment in 1928, and information recently supplied by the von Kleist family pinpoints the date as April 1, 1928; Nehring conversely states that it was January 1, 1929. From Breslau, von Kleist was once again transferred and posted as Chief of Staff of the 3rd Infantry Division (3. Division) in Berlin. Once again the date is debatable: Moll states simply 1929; Nehring says July 1, 1929; and information from the family places the assignment on October 1, 1928. Furthermore, Nehring states that this was a dual posting with von Kleist being assigned as Chef des Stabes of both the 3. Division and Wehrkreis III (Military District III) in Berlin.[16] On October 1, 1929, he was promoted to the rank of Oberst (Colonel). From his staff position, the new Oberst returned to a command position again at last — this time as Kommandeur of the 9th Infantry Regiment (Infanterie-Regiment 9) in Potsdam near Berlin. Data from the family dates the assumption of this new command on April 1, 1930, while Nehring says February 1, 1931 and Moll says merely 1931. Whatever the actual date, from this time forward until the end of his military career Ewald von Kleist would serve only in positions of actual command — never again returning to staff duties. Command of combat troops in the field was of course always the career purpose of Ewald von Kleist — in the tradition of so many professional soldiers who had borne the von Kleist name before him — and he would later realize that purpose to the ultimate degree possible as holder of the highest rank in the German Army.

Although almost all career military officers aspire — at least in their minds — to bridge the most difficult of all promotion obstacles and attain the rank of General, very few ever actually achieve that goal. For Ewald von Kleist the goal was realized January 1, 1932, with his promotion to Charakterisiert Generalmajor. The prefix ''Charakterisiert'' (usually abbreviated ''Char.'') literally means ''in the character of'', and denotes the German equivalent of a brevet rank. Officers so designated wore the insignia of their ''Charakterisiert'' rank, but remained junior on the official rank list to all other officers who held the identical rank without the ''Char.'' prefix. At the time of his promotion to Char. Generalmajor, von Kleist was ''jumped'' over several senior Obersten (Colonels).[17] For the benefit of American readers, the German rank of Generalmajor is equivalent to a Brigadier General. One month after this promotion, on February 1, Ewald von Kleist was appointed as Commander of the 2. Kavallerie-Division in Breslau, of which he had earlier been Chief of Staff for a short time.

Von Kleist did not remain in his ''Charakterisiert'' rank status for long. On October 1, 1932, he was promoted to the regular rank of Generalmajor. Continuing to move upward rapidly, he was promoted to Generalleutnant (equivalent to a Major General in the American system) on October 1, 1933.[18] Eight months earlier, on January 30, Adolf Hitler had been appointed Chancellor (Reichskanzler) of Germany by the aging President Paul von Hindenburg, and his National Socialist German Workers' Party (NSDAP) was busily at work consolidating its power over the government. Very quickly Generalleutnant Ewald von Kleist experienced what was probably his first ''close encounter'' with the intrigues of the new National Socialist regime. The occassion was the period immediately leading up to the infamous ''Night of the Long Knives'' on June 30, 1934, when SA-Stabschef Ernst Röhm and numerous others were eliminated in the purge of the key leadership of the SA. For some time, high tension had been brewing between the Reichswehr and the SA (Sturmabteilung — the ''Brownshirts'' or ''Stormtroopers'' of the NSDAP, a paramilitary organization which had served as Hitler's private army in the early days). Röhm, as Chief of Staff of the SA, had long wanted the SA to supplant the Reichswehr as the official military force in Germany. Needing the support of the regular armed forces to solidify his power, Adolf Hitler reached a decision to rid himself of Röhm and of key SA leaders who shared the dream of an SA ''people's army''. Toward this end, a combined conspiracy developed between the SS (directed by Reichsführer Heinrich Himmler and SS-Brigadeführer Reinhard Heydrich) and certain elements of the Reichswehr leadership (principally the pro-Hitler Generalmajor Walter von Reichenau). The objective was to create the illusion of an imminent SA uprising against the Reichswehr and the government. Heydrich and von Reichenau did their work so well that on June 24 the Army was placed on alert in expectation of action by the SA.[19] In Breslau, after receiving ''a flood of alarming reports about the SA's revolutionary intentions'', Ewald von Kleist moved to find out the truth; in the words of one writer, the stories of the SA's plans ''seemed so improbable'' to von Kleist that he ''spontaneously took a step which nearly ruined the plans of Reichenau and Heydrich''.[20] Generalleutnant von Kleist promptly met with SA-Obergruppenführer Edmund Heines (head of SA-Gruppe Schlesien, headquartered in Breslau) to obtain an explanation of the actual situation. From this confrontation, he found his doubts about the rumored ''revolution'' all the more reinforced. As von Kleist testified before the International Military Tribunal in Nuremberg after the war, he and Heines came to the joint suspicion ''that we. . .were being incited against one another by a third party — I thought of Himmler, and that many of the reports came from him.''[21] Von Kleist did not let the matter lie there. He immediately flew to Berlin to report his conclusions to General von Fritsch, Commander-in-Chief of the Army (Oberbefehlshaber d. Heeres). In the presence of General Ludwig Beck, Chief of the Army General Staff, he advised von Fritsch of his serious suspicions and the reasons for them. Von Fritsch summoned von Reichenau and had von Kleist repeat the story; Reichenau, knowing full well the truth of what he heard, merely passed it off with calm unconcern: ''That may be, but it's too late now.''[22] Shortly thereafter the SS moved against the SA and Röhm was dead. Among the many others to lose their lives was Edmund Heines, the SA leader with whom von Kleist had consulted in Breslau. The power of the SA was broken and that of the SS firmly established; Heydrich was promptly promoted to SS-Gruppenführer; the postion of the Reichwehr as ''arms bearer of the nation'' was reaffirmed; and von Reichenau was on his way to higher command in the Army. Ewald von Kleist's unexpected interjection of himself into the affair in what could have been a critical manner for the plotters surely made an impression on the National Socialist powers and their supporters in the Reichswehr, and very likely played no small role in what was to befall him in February 1938.

At some point in this general time period — either shortly before or shortly after the Röhm purge — von Kleist assumed command of Wehrkreis VIII and also VIII. Armeekorps at Breslau. These were essentially the same entity, Wehrkreis VIII referring to the military administrative district in Silesia and VIII. A.K. being the grouping of Army units stationed there. Again, as usual it seems, the dates are unclear and contradictory from source to source. Three authors that wrote of von Kleist's actions prior to the Röhm purge (Joachim Fest, Heinz Höhne, and John Toland) all indicate that he was Wehrkreis Commander at the time — i.e., prior to June 30, 1934. This in fact seems quite logical, since the Commander of a Military District would have had far more motivation and authority to concern himself with such a sensitive matter than would a Cavalry Division Commander. However, Nehring gives the beginning date as October 1, 1934 (three months following the purge). He states that von Kleist was Commander of ''Befehlsstelle Breslau'' (literally ''Command Post Breslau'') — further described as the ''disguise name'' (Tarnname) for VIII. Armeekorps — from that date through October 15, 1935, and concurrently Commanding General of VIII. A. K. through February 1938. Another source states that he became Commanding General of the Army Corps on May 21, 1935. Data supplied by the von Kleist family gives the date as October 1, 1935. Moll says 1936! At least this latter citation seems obviously erroneous, since the official German Army Rangliste (Rank List) for October 16, 1935 shows him as Commander of Wehrkreis VIII at that time.[23]

Contrary to the stereotype image many people conjure in their minds when they think of an "aristocratic Prussian General", Ewald von Kleist was a warm and human officer who was highly regarded by those under his command. He made a lasting impression on those who served with and under him, and retained their esteem. A typical manifestation of this regard was seen on March 31, 1936, on which date the 2nd Cavalry Division was disbanded. Von Kleist had commanded that Division for some three years (1932-1934). On the day the Division passed into history, its officers presented him with a beautiful etching depicting the city of Breslau. On the reverse of the etching were the signatures of the Division Commander and his staff, and the following inscription: "On the last day of its existence the 2nd Cavalry Division remembers with gratitude and loyalty its knightly old commander and offers to him the most obedient salute."[24] This honest tribute from his old command obviously meant much to the combat-tried Cavalryman, since he carefully preserved it and it was among the belongings he carried with him when the von Kleist family left Breslau as refugees in 1945.

On August 1, 1936, von Kleist was promoted to the rank of General der Kavallerie (General of Cavalry) — equivalent to the American rank of Lieutenant General. At this time he was still Commanding General of Wehrkreis VIII and of VIII. Armeekorps. Soon, however, his active military service was to come to a temporary end. In January 1938 came the well-known "Blomberg-Fritsch Crisis" which saw the removal from office of the two top officers of the German Army. Generalfeldmarschall Werner von Blomberg - Minister of War (Reichskriegsminister), Commander-in-Chief of the Armed Forces (Oberbefehlshaber der Wehrmacht), and the first Field Marshal of the Third Reich — was dismissed by Hitler. Also dismissed was Generaloberst Werner Freiherr von Fritsch, Commander-in-Chief of the Army (Oberbefehlshaber des Heeres), based upon a false morals charge fabricated by the Gestapo with the guidance of Himmler and Hermann Goering. Through this move Adolf Hitler assumed direct command of the Armed Forces, which in 1935 had been renamed from Reichswehr to Wehrmacht. Following the dismissals the Ministry of War (Reichskriegsministerium) was abolished and replaced by the High Command of the Wehrmacht (Oberkommando der Wehrmacht), with Hitler as Commander-in-Chief. Generaloberst Walter von Brauchitsch replaced von Fritsch as Commander-in-Chief of the Army and in February 1938 a number of senior Army officers were sent into mandatory retirement. Included among these was Ewald von Kleist. The exact reasons for these dismissals, and the manner in which the officers involved were chosen, is still not completely clear today. Author Telford Taylor attributes a dual purpose to the dismissals — to remove "the more aristocratic, religious, or outspokenly anti-Nazi officers", and "to retire enough generals to 'loosen up' the top of the ladder and make possible the promotion of several generals of definite pro-Nazi sympathies" (such as Reichenau, List, Busch, Guderian, and von Schobert).[25] Von Kleist appears to have fit all of the basic criteria for dismissal — aristocratic, religious, and basically anti-Nazi. Taylor describes him as an "old-line aristocrat" and a "strong monarchist and close to the Hindenburg family." Nehring attributes his discharge from active duty as being ordered "for political reasons" by Hitler. Moll states that he was removed because he was in opposition to the NSDAP, conducted himself "negatively" toward the Party, and "made no secret" of his attitude. The dismissal was made effective February 2, 1938. General von Kleist was not, however, retired on a permanent basis. He was placed in "zur Verfügung" status (abbreviated as z.V., and meaning literally "at disposal"), meaning that he was available for further duty and subject to recall. Despite the political implications of his retirement, Ewald von Kleist

was in no sense dismissed in disgrace or "under a cloud". On the day he retired, he was presented with a portrait photograph of Adolf Hitler bearing a personal handwritten inscription reading: "Herr General der Kavallerie von Kleist, with my best wishes — Adolf Hitler, Berlin on 28 Feb. 1938."[26] As a further honor, von Kleist continued to be carried on the rolls of the official Army Rangliste as if still on active duty, and was authorized to wear the uniform of the 8th Cavalry Regiment (Kavallerieregiment 8) with the insignia of a General.[27] He plainly considered the right to wear the Regimental uniform a significant honor, as reflected by the fact that he had made for his uniform special shoulder boards (Schulterstücke) with the braid of a General but with the golden-yellow underlay color (Waffenfarbe) of the German Cavalry. The regulation shoulder board underlay color for German Generals was red. In addition, he wore on his shoulder boards the metal numeral "8", denoting Kavallerieregiment 8. Following his recall to active service at the beginning of the Second World War, von Kleist continued to proudly wear this special insignia on his field uniform and on his white summer tunic until his promotion to the rank of Field Marshal.

For some eighteen months, Ewald von Kleist was able to enjoy the peaceful life of a country gentleman, husband, and father. Following his mandatory retirement, he acquired a beautiful plantation-like country estate at Weidebrück near Breslau which would be the von Kleist family home — until they were ultimately driven from it by the advance of the Russian Army into Silesia in 1945. During this retirement period his eldest son — also best known by the name of Ewald — followed his father's footsteps and became an officer in the German Cavalry. Young Ewald was commissioned as a Leutnant on September 1, 1938, and was assigned to Kavallerieregiment 9 at Fürstenwald (Spree). Very shortly thereafter, both father and son would find themselves participating in the German conquest of Poland. As the storm clouds of war once again began to form over Europe, the German Army found itself in a state of rapid buildup and mobilization for the coming conflict. As a part of this buildup, several senior retired officers — including a number of those involuntarily retired in the wake of the 1938 Blomberg-Fritsch Crisis and "purge" of the Army — found themselves recalled to active service. Among those recalled to duty in August 1939 was General der Kavallerie Ewald von Kleist. His high worth as a military leader again recognized — and soon to be proven beyond doubt in the conflagration of the Second World War — von Kleist found himself assigned as Commanding General of XXII Armeekorps (mot.). The 22nd Army Corps (Motorized) consisted of the 2nd and 5th Panzer Divisions and the 4th Light Division (4. leichte Division).[28] Thus the traditional cavalryman was to experience his first real taste of armored, mechanized warfare — a style of war which he was to quickly master, and in which he would excel. It is interesting to note that certain of von Kleist's key superior and subordinate officers in the Polish Campaign would continue to figure in the scene of subsequent campaigns with him as well. His Chief of Staff was Oberst Kurt Zeitzler, who would serve under von Kleist in the same capacity in France and the Balkans, and in Russia until April 1942. His immediate superior was Generaloberst Wilhelm List, Commanding General of 14th Army (14. Armee); von Kleist's Panzers would later serve under List in France and Yugoslavia, and again for a few months in 1942 in Russia. In Poland, his senior commander was Generaloberst Gerd von Rundstedt, Commanding General of Army Group South (Heeresgruppe Süd). Again a similar command relationship would exist between von Rundstedt and von Kleist in France and in Russia up until December 1941.

The invasion of Poland came close to a premature start. The attack was originally scheduled for the early morning hours of August 26, 1939, with all units of the invading forces under orders to automatically begin their advances at the designated time. However, a last-minute postponement occurred late on August 25 because of diplomatic maneuvering. Some difficulties were experienced in getting the cancellation order to the field units. Along the southern sector, according to Telford Taylor, "the motorized troops of Kleist's corps were stopped only by landing a staff officer in a Fieseler Storch (liaison) airplane on the frontier."[29] Despite the postponement order and the near "false start", the war itself was only briefly delayed. On September 1, 1939, the German invasion of Poland was launched with lightning reality, and with it World War II was born. Striking from Silesia through Slovakia into southern Poland, Ewald von Kleist's XXII Armeekorps played its role in the operation with effectiveness and vigor. Driving to the northwest through Tarnow and Tomaszow to the east of Lublin, his forces formed the right wing of List's advance. On September 17, they met up with advanced patrols of General Heinz Guderian's XIX Armeekorps which had driven southward from East Prussia into Poland and through Brest-Litowsk. This linkup formed an encirclement blocking any major retreat of Polish forces to the east, while the destruction of the Polish forces trapped between the armored "pincers" and Warsaw to the west was accomplished by other German commands. The siege of Warsaw (in which von Kleist did not participate) lasted until September 27, when its defenders surrendered. Adolf Hitler entered Warsaw on October 5, 1939 and reviewed a victory parade of the triumphant Wehrmacht.[30] Thus ended the first phase of the long war to come, and the first of many German victories before the eventual defeat and destruction of the Third Reich.

With the fall of Poland, the war temporarily entered a "quiet" period for the German Wehrmacht. It was a time of intensive planning and preparation for the greater struggles to come. In April Germany invaded Denmark and Norway, but von Kleist played no role in those actions. Instead, he found himself relocated to western Germany as the Wehrmacht regrouped for the invasion of France. The most decisive role in the first phase of the French Campaign was to be played by Army Group A (Heeresgruppe A), commanded by Generaloberst von Rundstedt. In the center of von Rundstedt's operational sector was the 12th Army under Generaloberst List. Subordinate to 12th Army was a newly-formed armored force under General der Kavallerie von Kleist, and it was von Kleist's role to spearhead the German drive from Belgium into France and all the way to the English Channel.

Von Kleist's forces constituted the largest formation of tanks which had yet been used together in warfare. The official designation of this new armored force was the Gruppe von Kleist (Group von Kleist)[31], although it has come to be better known as Panzergruppe Kleist (Panzer Group Kleist). Technically, and in many of the period sources, the command was still known as the XXII Army Corps (Motorized) — from which it was derived, and which had been led by van Kleist in Poland. Expanded and vastly increased in power, Panzergruppe Kleist consisted of the XIX Panzerkorps under General der Panzertruppe Heinz Guderian, the XLI Panzerkorps under General der Panzertruppe Georg-Hans Reinhardt, and the XIV Armeekorps (mot.) under General der Infanterie Gustav von Wietersheim. In all the Panzergruppe included five Panzer divisions and three Motorized Infantry divisions. Its armored strength was approximately 1,260 tanks out of the total of about 2,800 tanks available to the Germans at the beginning of the offensive.[32] The formations of these Panzers were poised opposite the frontier of Luxembourg in a mass which was over a hundred miles in depth from its head to its tail, and the tail lay almost fifty miles east of the river Rhine. Von Kleist himself vividly described the scale of this Panzer force in his own words after the war: "If this Panzer Group had advanced on a single road its tail would have stretched back to Koenigsberg in East Prussia, when its head was at Trier."[33]

The offensive began on May 10, 1940. Panzergruppe Kleist crossed through Luxembourg and drove into the "impassable" forests and hills of the Belgian Ardennes, brushing aside weak opposition from Belgian forces and French cavalry. Reaching the Maas (Meuse) River late on the 11th, the Panzers crossed the river into France on May 13. The details of the German successes in France are thoroughly documented in numerous references, and will not be dealt with here. However, it is interesting to hear of the French Campaign in the words of Ewald von Kleist himself, as spoken to B. H. Liddell Hart after the end of World War II. Hart quotes von Kleist verbatim as follows[34]: "My leading troops, after traversing the Ardennes, crossed the French frontier on May 12th. General Schmundt, the Führer's adjutant, came forward to see me that morning, and asked whether I would prefer to continue the advance at once, and tackle the Meuse, or wait until the infantry corps came up. I decided to make the attempt without loss of time. General Schmundt then said that the Führer would place at my disposal next day, the 13th, the maximum support from the Luftwaffe — including the whole of Richthofen's air corps of dive bombers. Detailed arrangements were settled at a conference on the evening of the 12th with General Sperrle, who flew up to see me for the purpose — my headquarters were then near Bertrix. During the day my leading troops had pushed through the wooded belt north of the Meuse, and had reached its southern edge, overlooking the river. That night the reserves closed up, ready for an advance in strength. On the morning of the 13th the infantry regiments of the armored divisions pushed down to the river bank. The Luftwaffe — about a thousand aircraft — appeared on the scene at midday. Crossings were achieved early in the afternoon — at two places near Sedan, by General Guderian's corps, and near Montherme, by General Reinhardt's corps. All three attempts were successful, but the one near Montherme proved rather more difficult than the others, mainly because of the difficult terrain and steeply winding route of approach.

"The opposition was not serious. That was fortunate, for my artillery had only fifty rounds per battery — as the ammunition columns had been delayed by the congestion on the roads through the Ardennes. By the evening of the 13th my armored divisions had established strong bridgeheads over the Meuse. The leading infantry corps only began to arrive on the 14th. Along the Meuse there was a moderate amount of fortification, in the way of pillboxes, but these were not properly armed. If the French troops here had been adequately equipped with anti-tank guns we should certainly have noticed it, as the majority of our tanks were of the early Mark I type, and thus very vulnerable! The French divisions in the sector were poorly armed, and of low quality. Their troops, as we repeatedly found, gave up the fight very soon after being subjected to air bombing or gunfire."

After crossing the Meuse, Panzergruppe Kleist turned westward and aimed for the Channel coast, meeting spasmodic resistance. However, fearing a heavy French counterattack, Hitler directed the Oberkommando der Wehrmacht (OKW) to order the advance halted until sufficient infantry could be brought up to support the Panzer spearhead. This order was relayed to Guderian by von Kleist on the night of May 15-16. However, Guderian — who was intoxicated with enthusiasm over his successes, and who considered von Kleist to be too reserved and cautious — failed to execute the stop order. Reacting to this disobedience, von Kleist appeared at Guderian's field headquarters on the morning of May 17 and soundly reproached him for his arbitrary actions. In a fit of hotheadedness which often typified his manner, Guderian offered his resignation — which von Kleist promptly accepted, much to Guderian's surprise! Generaloberst List was dispatched to calm the storm and, after making it clear to Guderian that the stop order had originated not with von Kleist but Hitler personally, allowed him to resume his command.[35]

Once the advance resumed, the spectacular German successes continued. Again let us hear more of the story from von Kleist himself, as quoted by Hart: "I was halfway to the sea when one of my staff brought me an extract from the French radio which said that the commander of their 6th Army on the Meuse had been sacked, and General Giraud appointed to take charge of the situation. Just as I was reading it, the door opened and a handsome French general was ushered in. He introduced himself with the words, 'I am General Giraud.' He told me how he had set out in an armored car to look for his Army, and had found himself in the midst of my forces far ahead of where he had expected them to be. My first encounter with the British was when my tanks came upon, and over-ran, an infantry battalion whose men were equipped with dummy cartridges, for field exercises."[36]

Panzergruppe Kleist reached the sea on May 20 and turned north to capture the Channel ports. By May 23, Gen. Reinhardt's XLI Panzerkorps was only twenty miles from Dunkirk and the German armor was in a postion to cut off the British Expeditionary Force from escape through that port. At this critical moment with a great victory within easy grasp, Hitler issued orders to stop the advance of the German ground forces on May 24 in order that the Luftwaffe could have the task of "finishing off" the enemy. The order made no sense to the Army generals, and especially not to von Kleist. He later told Hart: "I decided to ignore it, and to push on across the (Aire-St. Omer) Canal. My armored cars actually entered Hazebrouck, and cut off the British lines of retreat. I heard later that the British Commander-in-Chief, Lord Gort, had been in Hazebrouck at the time. But then came a more emphatic order that I was to withdraw behind the canal. My tanks were kept halted there for three days. After three days the ban was lifted, and the advance was resumed — against stiffening opposition. It had just begun to make headway when it was interrupted by a fresh order from Hitler — that my forces were to be withdrawn, and sent southward for the attack on the line that the remainder of the French Army had improvised along the Somme. It was left for the infantry forces which had come down from Belgium to complete the occupation of Dunkirk — after the British had gone."[37]

The first phase of the French Campaign had ended. In recognition of his outstanding leadership and the success of his Panzergruppe, Ewald von Kleist had — during the height of the advance — been awarded the Knight's Cross of the Iron Cross (Ritterkreuz des Eisernes Kreuzes) on May 15, 1940. At the time of this award, it was the highest German military award for bravery or command achieve-ment (with the exception of the Grand Cross of the Iron Cross, which was awarded only once during the Third Reich). He had received the Iron Cross 1st and 2nd Classes in World War I, and had received the 1939 Clasps (Spangen) to his Iron Crosses 1st and 2nd Classes in the Polish Campaign. It is also interesting to note that von Kleist had in-troduced a novel and distinctive type of military vehicle marking for his forces during the first phase in France. All tanks and other vehicles of Panzergruppe Kleist had been marked with a large white "K" for identification purposes. He continued to use this marking for the vehicles of his command through the remainder of the French Campaign, in the Balkans, and during the initial phases of the com-ing invasion of Russia. Heinz Guderian has been erroneously credited by some sources as having originated such markings, since he imitated von Kleist's idea and had the tanks of his own forces marked with a white "G". However, the "G" marking did not come into use until the second phase of the French Campaign when Guderian was separated from von Kleist's command and given his own Panzergruppe.

On June 5, 1940, the second and final phase of the conquest of France was launched. Panzergruppe Kleist now consisted of Gen. von Wietersheim's XIV Armeekorps (mot.) and XVI Armeekorps (mot.) under General der Kavallerie Erich Hoepner, a brilliant tank commander who would later be executed in 1944 for complicity in the July 20 plot to assassinate Hitler. Included in these forces were three Panzer divisions (3rd, 4th, and 10th), one Motorized Infantry division, the Motorized Infantry Regiment "Grossdeutschland", and the Leibstandarte-SS "Adolf Hitler"(mot.).[38] After initial failure to break out of the Somme bridgeheads at Peronne and Amiens, Panzergruppe Kleist was shifted to the area of Laon and promptly

began to once again enjoy swift victories. On June 24 the French signed an armistice at Compiegne, although minor fighting con-tinued until June 30. On June 29 the spearhead of Panzergruppe Kleist reached the border of Spain, marking the end of the geographical conquest of France. The French Army — considered by many to be the finest in the world up to this time — had been soundly crushed by Germany in a campaign lasting less than two months. Much of the German victory can be credited to Ewald von Kleist and the other officers and men of Panzergruppe Kleist. For his role in the triumph, von Kleist was promoted to the rank of Generaloberst (Colonel-General) on July 19, 1940.

In the Fall of 1940, Panzergruppe Kleist was officially rede-signated as Panzergruppe I (1st Panzer Group). Under the command of Generaloberst von Kleist, it found itself transferred to Bulgaria in early 1941 in preparation for the planned invasion of Russia. However, it was first to play a primary role in the Balkan Campaign. Germany launched a simultaneous invasion of both Yugoslavia and Greece on April 6, 1941. On April 8, von Kleist's Panzergruppe I smashed across the border from Bulgaria into Yugoslavia and drove northward toward the Yugoslav capital of Belgrade. His forces in-cluded three Panzer divisions and two Motorized Infantry divisions. Despite the very difficult terrain, Panzergruppe I pushed aside the enemy and captured Belgrade on April 12 — only four days after crossing the frontier — and linked with Panzers of the 2nd Army which had converged on the capital after driving southward from Hungary. Yugoslavia capitulated on April 17, and another campaign came to its swift conclusion. On April 23, the invasion of Greece also came to a quick end with the capitulation of the Greek Army. According to at least one source (but unsubstantiated in other available references) von Kleist moved into Athens on April 27 and Panzer divisions under his command moved into the Peloponnesos to inflict heavy casualties upon the evacuating British Expeditionary Corps before it escaped from Greece with most of its men but none of its heavy equipment.[39] On May 13, von Kleist was awarded the Grand Cross of the Hungarian Order of Merit with Swords in recognition of his key role in the Balkan Campaign (in which Hungarian forces had participated on a token scale).[40] Yet to come were his greatest victories and final defeat in the vastness of the Soviet Union.

Following the Balkan Campaign, Generaloberst von Kleist and his Panzergruppe I were moved to Rumania, and then on to eastern Poland for Operation Barbarossa — the invasion of the Soviet Union. Panzergruppe I was to form the armored spearhead of Generalfeld-marschall von Rundstedt's Army Group South, which had the objec-tive of occupying the Ukraine with its important agriculture and its vital industrial and oil complexes. The invasion was launched on June 22, 1941. Von Kleist played a leading roll in the southern sector of the Russian Campaign from the first day onward until his dismissal by Hitler at the end of March 1944 — commanding Panzergruppe I, then Panzerarmee I (1st Panzer Army), and finally Heeresgruppe A (Army Group A). The battle-by-battle history of the war in Russia is far too complex to be dealt with in any depth here. By following the photo captions in this book, the reader will have a chronological overview of the major highlights of that part of the Russian Campaign which involved von Kleist and his various com-mands. For a detailed basic study of the war in Russia, I would recommend Paul Carell's fine companion volumes — *Hitler Moves East* and *Scorched Earth* — as an excellent starting point. For our pur-poses here, I must largely limit the remaining pages to facts concern-ing von Kleist's career and personal life and to an effort to portray the character of the man through his own words and those of others.

After the war, Ewald von Kleist spoke in depth with noted British military writer B. H. Liddel Hart about the war in general and Russia in particular. Thanks to Hart, his comments and views have been preserved. Concerning the launching of Operation Barbarossa, von Kleist claimed that he was only told of the decision to invade Russia a short time before the actual attack. His comments were, in part, as follows: "It was the same with the other high commanders. We were told the Russian armies were about to take the offensive, and it was essential for Germany to remove the menace. It was explained to us that the Führer could not proceed with other plans while this threat loomed close, as too large a part of the German forces would be pinned down in the east keeping guard. It was argued that attack was the only way for us to remove the risks of a Russian attack. I believe Jodl was opposed to Hitler's conclusion, as well as Brauchitsch and Halder...We did not underrate the Red Army, as is commonly imagined. The last German military attache in Moscow, General Köstring — a very able man — had kept us well informed about the state of the Russian Army. But Hitler refused to credit his information. Hopes of victory were largely built on the prospect that the invasion would produce a political upheaval in Russia. Most of us generals realized beforehand that, if the Russians chose to fall back, there was very little chance of achieving a final victory without the help of such an upheaval. Too high hopes were built on the belief that Stalin would be overthrown by his own people if he suffered heavy defeats. . . . There were no preparations for a prolonged struggle. Everything was based on the idea of a decisive result before the autumn."[41]

Contrary to popular belief, the German tank forces thrown into Russia in 1941 were far inferior numerically to those of the Red Army. Von Kleist's own Panzergruppe I had only some 600 tanks. Commenting on this to Hart, he stated: "That will probably seem incredible to you, but it was all we could assemble after the return of the divisions from Greece. Budenny's Army Group, facing us in the south, had some 2,400 tanks. Apart from surprise, we depended for success simply on the superior training and skill of the troops. These were decisive assets until the Russians gained experience."[42]

By the end of September 1941, the Ukrainian capital of Kiev had been captured — along with over 660,000 Russian prisoners — in a great encirclement maneuver executed by von Kleist's Panzergruppe I and Guderian's Panzergruppe II. Moving eastward, von Kleist struck across the Dnieper River at Dnepropetrovsk and Zaporozhye and then drove south to Mariupol on the Sear of Azov. On October 6, 1941, his Panzer Group had been enlarged and upgraded to Panzerarmee I (1st Panzer Army). After a temporary halt to operations due to autumn mud, his forces moved on toward Rostov — gateway city to the Caucasus. Rostov was taken by advance German units in November, but temporarily lost again by a heavy Russian counteroffensive in December. With the vast Ukraine and much of the Donets Basin area under its control, the German Army regrouped for a renewed offensive in the coming spring. Germany had failed to achieve the expected collapse of the Soviet Union and quick victory. In the view of von Kleist, "The main cause of our failure was that winter came early that year, coupled with the way the Russians repeatedly gave ground rather than letting themselves be drawn into a decisive battle such as we were seeking."[43]

On February 17, 1942, Generaloberst von Kleist became the 72nd German soldier to receive the Oakleaves (Eichenlaub) to the Knight's Cross of the Iron Cross. This award recognized his outstanding leadership and the achievements of his troops in conquering the Ukraine. Many more achievements were soon to come. With the end of the harsh Russian winter, he initiated what has been described as "an offensive which has no parallel in terms of daring and strategic concept."[44] In May 1942, his Panzer Army — operating together with the German 17th Army — executed "Operation Fridericus" and encircled an enormous force of the Red Army south of the city of Kharkov. The Russians, who themselves had intended to encircle the Germans, lost the bulk of twenty-nine divisions and their armor was routed; the German Army captured over 230,000 Russian soldiers and captured or destroyed over 1,500 tanks and 2,000 guns. By July, 1st Panzer Army had recaptured Rostov and was poised to cross the Don River into the Caucasus. Earlier, in June, Ewald von Kleist had been awarded the Commander Class of the Italian Military Order of Savoy by Mussolini as further recognition of his conquest of the Ukraine and his leadership of the Italian Expeditionary Corps in Russia (which was operationally attached to 1st Panzer Army).[45]

In August 1942 von Kleist's forces crossed the Don into the Caucasus and drove across the Kuban Steppe toward the oilfields to the southeast. Within the month he had captured the oilfields at Maikop and was heading for the great fields at Grozny. The Terek River was reached by August 30, but this river marked the limit of the Caucasus offensive and Grozny remained barely beyond reach. Von Kleist continued his efforts to advance in force beyond the Terek until November 1942, but success was not to be had. He described the situation to Hart in these words: "The primary cause of our failure was shortage of petrol. The bulk of our supplies had to come by rail from the Rostov bottleneck, as the Black Sea route was considered unsafe. A certain amount of oil was delivered by air, but the total which came through was insufficient to maintain the momentum of the advance, which came to a halt just when our chances looked best. But that was not the ultimate cause of the failure. We could still have reached our goal if my forces had not been drawn away bit by bit to help the attack at Stalingrad. Besides part of my motorized troops, I had to give up the whole of my flak corps and all of my air force except the reconnaissance squadrons. That subtraction contributed to what, in my opinion, was a further cause of the failure. The Russians suddenly concentrated a force of 800 bombers on my front, operating from airfields near Grozny. Although only about a third of these bombers were serviceable, they sufficed to put a brake on my resumed advance, and it was all the more effective because of my lack of fighters and of flak."[46]

Von Kleist continued to describe the Caucasus situation as follows: "The Russians brought reserves round from the southern Caucasus and also from Siberia. These developed a menace to my flank here, which was so widely stretched that the Russian cavalry could always penetrate my outposts whenever they chose. This flank concentration of theirs was helped by the railway that the Russians built across the Steppes, from Astrakhan southward. It was roughly laid, straight over the level plain without any foundation. Efforts to deal with the menace by wrecking the railway proved useless, for as soon as any section of the railway was destroyed a fresh set of rails was quickly laid down, and joined up. My patrols reached the shores of the Caspian, but that advance carried us nowhere, for my forces in this quarter were striking against an intangible foe. As time passed and the Russian strength grew in that area the flanking menace became increasingly serious."[47]

As the German advance through the Soviet Union progressed through 1941 and 1942, large numbers of Soviet citizens welcomed the Germans as liberators from the harsh regime of Josef Stalin and Communism. This situation was especially prevalent in the Ukraine (which was highly nationalistic and desired independence), in the Crimea, and in the Caucasus. Cossacks and Tartars in the Caucasus and the Crimea flocked to the German side with high hopes that they could win their freedom, taking up arms against the Red regime. Unfortunately for the German cause and for the Cossacks and others who joined hands with the invaders, the political leadership of Germany — adhering to the Nazi philosophy that these peoples were racially inferior and untrustworthy — failed to exploit this opportunity. As the German Army moved deeper and deeper into Russia, harsh and repressive civilian administrations were imposed in the areas behind the front lines. The Ukraine suffered especially under the obnoxious and arrogant Gauleiter Erich Koch, who was appointed Reichskommissar for the Ukraine (the senior administrator for the region). A planned Reichskommissar for the Caucasus never materialized, due to the short-lived German control of that area. Many of the senior German Army commanders in Russia — and especially Ewald von Kleist — had the wisdom to recognize the foolishness of the Nazi occupational policies and did what they could to counteract them wherever and whenever possible.

Von Kleist particularly realized the need for earning the trust and cooperation of the local populace in Russia. In receiving General der Kavallerie Ernst Köstring (who had just been appointed as "Deputy General for the Caucasus" because of his outstanding knowledge of Russia) at the headquarters of Army Group A at Stavropol in September 1942, he tellingly remarked: "These vast spaces depress me. And these vast hordes of people. We're lost if we don't win them over."[48] Later that same month, von Kleist was visited by another cavalry officer and expert on the Russians — Oberst (later Generalleutnant) Helmuth von Pannwitz. Von Pannwitz had set for himself the goal of establishing a genuine combat formation of Cossacks within the German Army to combat communism. Fighting against the shortsighted political opposition to his idea, von Pannwitz had already gained the support of General der Infanterie Kurt Zeitzler (newly-appointed Army Chief of Staff and former Chief of Staff to von Kleist in France and Russia) for his ideas. After a visit to the Don, Kuban, and Terek areas of the Caucasus to study the Cossack situation there, and he had reported to von Kleist to pass on his findings. Von Kleist agreed with von Pannwitz in the view that the desire of the freedom-loving Cossacks to regain their in- dependence by fighting along side the German Army against com- munism should be strongly encouraged. He told Pannwitz that he had submitted such a proposal to the OKH (Army High Command), together with a recommendation that Pannwitz himself be designated to command the new Cossack formation. Thanks in no small part to von Kleist's proposals, he was eventually allowed to put his plans into action.[49] Unfortunately again for the Germans, it was too little too late. And most unfortunately for von Pannwitz personal- ly and for the Cossacks he loved, he and most of the Cossacks were executed by the Soviets following the war — having been turned over to Stalin by the British and Americans.

In early September 1942, Generalfeldmarschall List had been relieved of command of Army Group A (which included von Kleist's 1st Panzer Army) and Adolf Hitler had assumed personal opera- tional command of the Army Group. Von Kleist became the senior Army officer in the Caucasus, and shortly thereafter he was officially appointed by Hitler as Commander-in-Chief of Army Group A (effec- tive November 22, 1942). By that time, the German military situation in the Caucasus was already hopeless. In January 1943, a massive Russian counteroffensive rapidly drove Army Group A almost com- pletely out of the Caucasus, and it was only von Kleist's brilliant tac- tics during that retreat that prevented the annihilation of the German forces. Army Group A was essentially split into two parts for the retreat. The bulk of 1st Panzer Army retreated northward from the Terek back to the Don, covering a distance of 375 miles in thirty days, where it passed into operational control of Generalfeld- marschall Erich von Manstein's Army Group South. The remainder of Army Group A — primarily the 17th Army — withdrew across the Kuban bridgehead onto the Taman peninsula in only four weeks' time. Of the withdrawal, Paul Carell writes as follows: "This retreat too was an achievement almost without parallel in military history. A chapter in the war, marked by gallantry, dedication, and readiness for sacrifice on the part of officers and men, and not with weapons only but equally so with spades, alongside horses and mules. Here more than anywhere else did the German Wehrmacht reap the benefits of its progressive, modern structure, its lack of social bar- riers and class prejudice. The German Army was the only army in the world in which officers and men shared the same food. The of- ficer was not only the leader in battle but also the 'foreman', a 'trooper with epaulettes', whose unhesitating participation in carry- ing loads or freeing stuck vehicles set an example which conquered fatigue. In no other way could the adventure of this great retreat have succeeded."[50]

On February 1, 1943, Ewald von Kleist was promoted to Generalfeldmarschall (Field Marshal, commonly abbreviated GFM), the highest rank in the German Army, for his exceptional leadership during this most difficult of situation. B. H. Liddel Hart states of that promotion: "He was promoted to field-marshal for his achievement in conducting that retreat without serious loss, and it would seem to have been better earned than many who have gained their baton for offensive successes, as is the normal rule. For it is difficult to think of any retreat in history that has extricated an army from such a dangerous position under such extraordinary difficulties — with the handicap of distance multiplied by winter, and then again by the pressure of superior forces pressing down on his flank and rear."[51]

Von Kleist described the great retreat in his own words to Hart: "Although our offensive in the Caucasus had reached its abortive end in November, 1942, when stalemate set in, Hitler insisted on our staying in that exposed forward position, deep in the mountains. At the beginning of January a serious danger to my rear flank developed from an attack which the Russians delivered from Elista westwards past the southern end of Lake Manych. This was more serious than the Russian counterattacks on my forward position, near Mozdok. But the greatest danger of all came from the Russian advance from Stalingrad, down the Don towards Rostov, far in my rear. When the Russians were only 70 kilometers from Rostov, and my armies were 650 kilometers east of Rostov, Hitler sent me an order that I was not to withdraw under any circumstances. That looked like a sentence of doom. On the next day, however, I received a fresh order — to retreat, and bring away everything with me in the way of equipment. That would have been difficult enough in any case, but became much more so in the depths of the Russian winter. The protection of my flank from Elista back to the Don had originally been entrusted to the Rumanian Army Group under Marshal Antonescu. Antonescu himself did not arrive on the scene, thank God! Instead, the sector was placed under Manstein, whose Army Group South included part of the Rumanian forces. With Manstein's help, we succeeded in withdrawing through the Rostov bottleneck before the Russians could cut us off. Even so, Manstein was so hard pressed that I had to send some of my own divisions to help him in holding off the Rus- sians who were pushing down the Don towards Rostov. The most dangerous time of the retreat was the last half of January."[52]

Although primarily concerned with saving his own troops, GFM von Kleist did not forget those citizens of the Caucasus who had taken the side of the Germans against communism. He personally established a "Caucasus Refugee Staff" to organize the retreat of the civilians, and shortly thereafter tens of thousands of Caucasian natives — primarily Cossacks — began their own retreat from the ad- vancing Red Army. Many were cut off and fell into the hands of the Soviets, and Reichskommissar Koch threatened to seize the horses of any Cossacks who tried to pass through the Ukraine to safety. Despite all these hardships, the surviving Cossacks and their families eventually managed to reach northern Italy and the end of their march. Following a separate line of retreat, numerous Kalmucks moved through the Ukraine and eventually reached Neuhammer in Silesia — the area of von Kleist's old Wehrkreis VIII command.[53]

Throughout the Russian Campaign — in both good days and bad — Ewald von Kleist steadfastly deported himself in the manner of an honorable gentleman. His deep religious beliefs, combined with his courage as a professional officer, caused him to make every effort within his power to see that just and decent measures were applied to Russians and Germans alike. Many examples can be cited. For in- stance, he strongly opposed the forced labor conscriptions carried out in Russia under the direction of Gauleiter Fritz Sauckel during 1943. Author Alan Clark comments on that opposition in a revealing way: "Kleist even went so far as to draft a special memorandum ordering that recruitment be solely on a voluntary basis — and took steps to see that 'voluntary' meant what it said. This drew an im- mediate howl of protest from Koch, who made Sauckel send Hitler a telegram: 'Unfortunately several Commanding Generals in the East have forbidden the labor conscription of men and women in the conquered Soviet territories — for political reasons, as Gauleiter Koch informs me. (This was a lie.) My Führer! I ask you to countermand these orders so as to enable me to carry out my assignment."[54] In another interesting citation, even Dr. Josef Goebbels confirms von Kleist's compassionate actions: "Field Marshals Manstein and Kleist have introduced somewhat more humane treatment of the inhabitants in the regions that have again come under military administration because of our retreat. The measures of Koch, which could not be executed anyway, were modified considerably."[55] Illustrating the point still further, Jürgen Thorwald has described a scene which unfolded during a June 1943 visit of Reichsminister Alfred Rosenberg and Reichskommissar Koch to von Kleist's headquarters near Dnepropetrovsk. Addressing Rosenberg, von Kleist is quoted as saying: "Herr Minister, I am most grateful for this chance to speak to you personally. There is one matter that concerns us soldiers deeply. Unfortunately, we have been forced to recognize, by bitter experience, that we are all in hopeless positons unless there is a revision of policy in the Ukraine and toward the Ukrainians. . . ."

In his typical manner, Koch interjected: "It is well known, Herr Feldmarschall, that you regard the situation with an extremely dangerous degree of pessimism. I have long had the impression that you lack faith in the Führer, as well as the confidence essential for a soldier, and without which he is probably in the wrong place. I have been informed by the Führer personally that the real situation is rather different from your view of it." Kleist then responded simply by saying, "I would only wish, Herr Gauleiter, that your optimism might prove of some practical comfort to us here." Following the confrontation, Koch said to Rosenberg of von Kleist: "There's another one who's just about due."[56]

It is obvious that Ewald von Kleist refused to be intimidated by the NSDAP and by the bureaucracy in situations which reduced many other competent generals — those who placed career considerations above any personal standards of honor and fairness — to the status of mere "yes men". His strict devotion to a code that required proper conduct both by himself and those under his command never faltered, despite the potential danger it must have frequently posed for his career and even for his personal safety. Men like Koch and Sauckel could never be taken lightly. It was still more dangerous to stand up in the face of the awesome power of Heinrich Himmler and his SS, but even the SS could not induce von Kleist to abandon his code. Certainly he faced the severest of these situations in Russia, where the vulgar and brutal administrative excesses of Koch and Sauckel were matched with the terror of the SS-Einsatzgruppen ("Special Mission" Operations Groups), which carried out executions of countless communist officials, Jews, and others in the occupied areas. Under Hitler's orders, the Army had full authority in the actual combat zones (i.e. in operational zones at or near the front lines), but in the occupied areas to the rear of the front the SS and Police held full sway. Von Kleist and other military commanders could thus do little to restrain the SS behind the front lines, but he clearly did not tolerate brutality in the areas he did control. In *The Trial of the Germans*, Eugene Davidson states as follows: "Field commanders took action when they heard rumors of the Einsatz squads' executions. Field Marshal von Kleist, for example, called the Higher SS and Police Leaders to him as soon as he had heard such a report and told them he would permit no excesses in his area of command."[57]

While the SD and the SS-Einsatzgruppen committed many inhuman acts in Russia, the regular combat arm of the SS — the Waffen-SS — fought side by side with the Army in the field and were, on the whole nothing more or less than brave and loyal soldiers. At various times during the Russian Campaign, Ewald von Kleist had under his command some of the most famous of the Waffen-SS combat units — including the Leibstandarte-SS "Adolf Hitler" and the SS-Panzer-Grenadier-Division "Wiking". He enjoyed a close working relationship in the field with such Waffen-SS commanders as Sepp Dietrich of the Leibstandarte. However, occasional problems did arise because the SS generals had a tendency (no doubt because their organization was independent from the Wehrmact other than for operations in the field) to frequently disregard or exceed the Army's orders. As a professional soldier of the old school, von Kleist did not stand still for such "independence". In a typical instance, the "Wiking" division had exceeded its instructions during the course of an offensive, and its commander quickly received the following order by radio from von Kleist in response to his insubordination: "The commander of the 'Viking' division is 1: to be informed that the Army will not have positions occupied contrary to orders; 2: to report how it comes about that, without reporting the fact, he has occupied a position other than that expressly ordered by Corps Headquarters."[58]

While von Kleist's Heeresgruppe A was evacuating from the Caucasus in early 1943, the German 6th Army was being destroyed to the north at Stalingrad. After the loss of the 6th Army, it was rebuilt from scratch and would later come under the command of GFM von Kleist. As 1943 progressed, the German Army saw its dreams of Russian conquest wither and die. Despite various and sometimes spectacular local counteroffensives and temporary victories by the Wehrmacht, the German cause in Russia was lost. Gradually the Army fell back all along the Eastern Front. In September 1943, von Kleist took command of the reconstituted 6th Army in the southern Ukraine. His Heeresgruppe A now consisted of the 6th Army in the Ukraine and the 17th Army in the Crimea. As of October of that year, 6th Army had 13 German divisions and 2 Rumanian divisions, and 17th Army had only 3 German divisions and 7 quite unreliable Rumanian divisions with which to hold the whole of the Crimea. Stripped of most of his armor after losing his 1st Panzer Army to Army Group South in February, von Kleist's command now included only 83 tanks and 98 self-propelled assault guns. Against him the Red Army had massed some 45 rifle divisions, 3 tank corps, 2 guards mechanized corps, 2 guards cavalry corps, and 400 artillery batteries — with some 800 tanks.[59] Against such overwhelming odds there could be but one final outcome.

By December 1943, Heeresgruppe A was desperately holding along the lower stretches of the Dnieper River. By March 20, 1944, it had been beaten back to the Nikolayev area on the Bug. By March 30, GFM von Kleist had removed his headquarters back to Tiraspol on the lower Dnestr. GFM von Manstein, commanding Army Group South, was far to the northwest in his own new headquarters at Lvov. It was the final day of command for both men. On that date — March 30, 1944 — Hitler had both Field Marshals brought from the front to Berchtesgaden aboard his personal Condor aircraft. He presented each with the Swords (Schwertern) to the Knight's Cross of the Iron Cross, and relieved them of their commands. The obvious reason for this action was of course the German retreats in Russia, and Hitler's mistaken (and desperate) idea that men who would "stand firm" were needed. In von Manstein's case, he had furthermore been openly abrasive and abrupt with Hitler on several occasions, thus earning the Führer's personal dislike. Von Kleist had been more subtle with his Commander-in-Chief, but had equally failed to be the kind of "yes man" Hitler appreciated. Military historian E. F. Ziemke points out the following as some of the factors that contributed to von Kleist's dismissal: "Kleist had not engaged in any such dramatic encounter with Hitler, but he had consistently opposed him on the question of holding the Crimea and at the end had threatened to take matters into his own hands to get Sixth Army away from the Bug. In November 1943 he had proposed that Hitler devote himself mainly to internal and foreign policy and, in the style of World War I, create a First Quartermaster General of the Wehrmacht who would run the war on the Eastern Front and have strong advisory powers in the other theaters."[60]

Following his dismissal, von Kleist returned briefly to his Army Group A headquarters to attend to the formal transfer of command to the new Army Group Commander-in-Chief — Generaloberst Ferdinand Schörner (himself later to become a Field Marshal). Very shortly before his death in 1973, Schörner described the scene in a letter to General Walther Nehring: "I received the most powerful impression of von Kleist as a man and character on April 2, 1944 . . ., as I had to take over supreme command of his Army Group . . . . The unpleasant circumstances of this discharge, just as von Manstein for Model . . ., were well known. The soldierly deportment of Field Marshal Kleist appeared so much more remarkable and noble, uttering no word of anger or bitterness . . ., but quietly and calmly bearing his fate in an exemplary way. Never will I forget these words, with which he received me: 'Schörner, with your arrival you are the Commander-in-Chief of the Army Group. I am at your disposal.' At that time Field Marshal von Kleist was ten years my senior in service and age, quite apart from his superior position and importance . . . . The farewell was touching. Von Kleist had tears in his eyes as he wished me good luck; he still found the departure from his Army Group to be genuinely difficult."[61]

With the dismissal from command, Ewald von Kleist was reassigned to the OKH (Army High Command) in the same "z.V." — "at disposal"—status he had held following his first retirement in 1938. However the war would last barely another year, and he would never again be recalled to active duty. Retiring to his estate near Breslau, he would perform no further military duties aside from issuing the official certificates awarding the Kuban Shield (Kubanschild) decoration to his former troops in recognition of their bravery and sacrifices during the retreat from the Caucasus. He lived quietly with his wife at Weidebrück until early 1945, when the approach of the Red Army to Breslau forced them to emigrate to the tiny town of Mitterfels near Krenzkirchen in lower Bavaria. As the Russians moved against Breslau, his older son Ewald — who remained behind on active army duty — destroyed the family home with explosives to keep it from Russian hands.

At this point, a clarification of an oft-repeated historical inaccuracy is merited. In numerous books dealing with the period, it has been erroneously reported that GFM Ewald von Kleist was a participant of long standing in various conspiracies against Adolf Hitler and his regime. Even so widely acclaimed a source as Shirer's *The Rise and Fall of the Third Reich* perpetuates this falsehood. Shirer has von Kleist journeying secretly to England in August 1938 to warn Churchill and others of German intentions to invade Czechoslovakia, and also bringing back a secret letter from Churchill to Beck, Halder, and other anti-Hitler generals. Such a trip did take place, and it was made by a man named Ewald von Kleist. However, the man involved was Ewald von Kleist-Schmezin — a relative of our subject, but a member of a different branch of the large von Kleist family. This same Ewald von Kleist, together with his son Heinrich (a German Infantry officer, again having the same name as the younger son of GFM von Kleist), were involved in anti-Hitler circles for many years and were involved in plans to assassinate Hitler in 1944. It is fairly easy to understand the confusion here, given the duplication of names. The book *Hitler's Generals and their Battles* even goes so far off the track as to state the following specifically about GFM von Kleist: "Kleist was shelved by Hitler in 1944, but continued to plot against the Führer, an activity he had been involved with since before the war. Kleist was later taken into custody by the Gestapo."[62] Again, this statement properly pertains to Ewald von Kleist-Schmezin, and not to Field Marshal Ewald von Kleist. GFM von Kleist was clearly opposed to the policies of the NSDAP and to most of the ideas Hitler represented, but he pursued his opposition openly and legally through his official actions and his personal deportment — not secretly as a plotter or conspirator. Always true to his oath of loyalty as a German officer, his code of honor and his religious faith would not have allowed involvement in any covert plot to overthrow the government of his country or to assassinate its head of state.

On April 25, 1945, a military police patrol of the U.S. 26th Infantry Division found GFM von Kleist at his refugee home in Mitterfels and arrested the retired officer. According to Moll, von Kleist initially refused to submit to arrest despite being threatened with a pistol, but finally ceased his resistance after his wife entered the room and brought calm to the tense situation.[63] After being allowed to pack his personal belongings, he was taken away into captivity — a captivity from which he would never be allowed to return. From that point forward, he spent the remainder of his life in various camps and prisons as a prisoner of war and so-called "war-criminal". According to Konteradmiral a.D. Hasso von Bredow, a fellow inmate with him until March 1953, von Kleist was held in a total of 27 different prisons between 1945 and his death.[64] Having surrendered to the Americans, he remained in the hands of the Western Allies for little over a year. Most of his initial period of confinement was at No. 11 P.O.W. Camp at Trent Park in England — a camp for senior German officers. His fellow prisoners there included such notable men as GFM von Rundstedt, General der Panzertruppe Hasso von Manteuffel, and Luftwaffe Generaloberst Kurt Student. Von Kleist remained at Trent Park until August 31, 1946, when — to the great discredit of the British and American authorities, and for obvious political expediency — he was handed over for extradition to Yugoslavia to be tried for alleged war crimes. On September 7, 1946, while in Vienna en route to Belgrade for trial, he wrote the last letter he would be allowed to send to his family for the coming eight and one half years. That letter, which is still treasured by the von Kleist family, reads: "My dear ones! You will have seen in the newspapers that I have been brought to Belgrade. Do not worry! The reason is puzzling to me, the more I reflect on it. I have the best conscience, a clean shield, and trust in God. But also, based upon my handling up to now, I am confident that it will turn out right for me. My large baggage is still in England. I hope that Rundstedt will attend to it. He knew nothing of my fate when I left him. God protect you all! Thanks for your love! E."[65]

Sadly indeed for Ewald von Kleist and for his family, his faith and his personal knowledge that he had conducted himself with honor and humanity throughout the war were not any protection from his new communist captors. Tried in Belgrade for alleged war crimes, he was convicted and sentenced to 15 years imprisonment. The exact "crimes" for which he was tried are unknown, but they very likely were little more or less than his key role in the swift military conquest of Yugoslavia in April 1941. In any event, he would remain in Yugoslavia for only a relatively short time. As a final and eventually fatal blow, Ewald von Kleist was turned over to the Russians in 1948. It is unclear whether he was subjected to a further trial by the Russians, but in all probability this did happen. According to fellow prisoner Konteradmiral von Bredow, he was held accused by the Soviets as a war criminal for having "alienated through mildness and kindness the population" of the Soviet Union during the war — i.e., for having treated the Soviet citizenry with more compassion than they had received from their own government, thus causing them to take sides with the German invaders![66]

Upon his removal to Russia, von Kleist was initially confined in the Lubjanka Prison at Moscow. Eventually he was transferred to the Soviet prison camp for German generals at Wladimir, approximately 300 kilometers east of Moscow. Since his extradition to Belgrade in late 1946, his family had received no word of his fate or his whereabouts. Finally, in March 1954, he was allowed to begin a very limited correspondence once again. Beginning at that point, his Russian captors allowed him to write and to receive one postcard-type letter each month. Not knowing the fate or whereabouts of his family (just as they had not known his), he sent his first postcard in care of friends in north Germany. Upon finally relocating his loved ones, he was then able to correspond directly with them for the brief remainder of his life. During this short period, he was also allowed to receive packages containing various articles for his personal use — such as food, coffee, and cigars — and photographs from home. Through the postcards, he was able to learn of the 1952 marriage of his younger son, Heinrich, and of the birth of his first grandchild (Ulrike von Kleist) in 1953. The last postcard he wrote to Germany was dated September 5, 1954. By means of the reply to that card, he may have learned of the birth of his second grandchild (Christoph Ewald von Kleist) on September 15 of that year.[67] If so, this would have been the last good news he received from home, for Generalfeldmarschall Ewald von Kleist died in solitary confinement at Camp Wladimir on October 15, 1954 — the only German Field Marshal to die in the hands of the Soviets. In January 1955, his widow received official notice of his death in the form of a formal death certificate issued by the Military Administration of the Wladimir District. Official cause of the Field Marshal's death was given as "general arteriosclerosis and hypertension". The death certificate was forwarded to Frau von Kleist by the East German Ministry of Foreign Affairs, acting on behalf of the Soviet Embassy in East Germany.[68] So far as is known, this is the only instance in which the USSR provided the family of a German soldier with a death certificate after the soldier died in Soviet hands. It seems reasonable to conclude that this special "courtesy" was an effort to quiet natural suspicions about the cause of death of the highest-ranking German officer to die in Russia.

In January 1956, Rittmeister a.D. Ewald von Kleist — older son of the Field Marshal — returned to Germany from over 10 years of Russian imprisonment in Siberia. Four months later, GFM von Kleist's mother died at the age of 100. His beloved wife Gisela died in May 1958, having survived her spouse for a short four years. In 1971 death claimed his only sister, Anna Marie Hertha von Kleist. Ewald von Kleist's two sons, Ewald and Heinrich, passed away in 1976 and 1973 respectively. Despite the passing of so many loved ones, however, the name and memory of the gentle old soldier live on in the person of eight grandchildren — three by his older son (Andrea, Heinrich, and Regine), and five by his younger son (Ulrike, Ewald, Elisabeth, Gisela, and Nicole). With such a human legacy, and with his personal code of honor unbroken to the last, any man can rightfully rest in peace with his God.

In conclusion, there would seem to be no finer epitaph for Generalfeldmarschall Paul Ludwig Ewald von Kleist — cavalryman, Panzer commander, devoted husband and father, and uncomplicated man of honest faith — than the following words of author Otto Moll: "HE WAS A SOLDIER OF THE OLD SCHOOL, AN OFFICER IN THE SENSE OF THE BEST TRADITION."

von Kleist

Ewald von Kleist as Oberleutnant of Hussars. (Christa von Kleist)

Oberleutnant von Kleist at the head of a patrol of lancers. This photograph was probably taken circa 1912, when he was assigned to Husarenregiment Nr. 14. (Christa von Kleist)

Von Kleist leads a reconnaissance probe, probably on the Eastern Front against Imperial Russian forces circa 1915. He is the officer pointing with the riding crop. (Christa von Kleist)

Rittmeister Ewald von Kleist as Squadron Chief with the 1. Leibhusaren-Regiment. (Christa von Kleist)

Rittmeister von Kleist as Ia (Chief of Staff) of the Garde-Kavallerie-Division, circa 1917. (Christa von Kleist)

In 1922, Ewald von Kleist was posted as an Instructor of Tactics on the staff of the Cavalry School at Hannover. He was promoted to Major in 1923. This photograph was probably taken on the school's parade and training field. (Christa van Kleist)

Von Kleist as Oberst and Commander of Infanterie-Regiment 9 (Berlin), 1931. He wears the numeral "9" on his shoulder boards, denoting the Regiment. This exceptional studio portrait by Transocean G.m.b.H. Berlin, still mounted in its original protective folder, was among the personal belongings of General-feldmarschall von Kleist confiscated in June 1945 by U.S. Army Intelligence personnel.

Ewald von Kleist with his two sons. To his right is his younger boy Heinrich, and to his left is his son Ewald. Von Kleist was a loving father dedicated to his family. (Christa von Kleist)

Another view of von Kleist with his sons. The family German shepherd relaxes in the background. (Christa von Kleist)

Gisela von Kleist, wife of Ewald von Kleist. Born Gisela Wachtel in 1889, she and Ewald von Kleist were married on Oct. 18, 1910 at Hannover. Frau von Kleist survived her husband by less than four years, passing away at Westert, W. Germany in May 1958. (Christa von Kleist)

Sept. 16, 1932. Von Kleist as Generalmajor and Commander of the 2. Kavallerie-Division at Breslau. This photograph was taken during war games near Frankfurt in which the 1st and 2nd Cavalry Divisions were pitted against the 3rd Infantry Divison. Von Kleist was commander of the "Red" forces during the maneuvers. (Christa von Kleist)

Another photograph taken during the war games near Frankfurt on Sept. 16, 1932. Generalmajor von Kleist (holding map) discusses the operation with Generalleutnant Fedor von Bock (wearing Pour le Merite decoration), Commander of the 1st Cavalry Division. Both Bock and von Kleist later achieved the rank of Generalfeldmarschall, highest rank in the German Army. (Christa von Kleist)

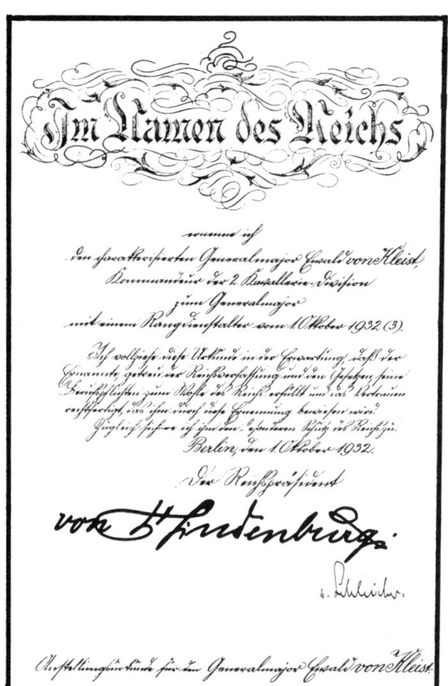

Official document promoting Ewald von Kleist from Char. Generalmajor to Generalmajor, effective October 1, 1932. At this time he was serving as Commander of the 2nd Cavalry Division at Breslau. The document is signed by President von Hindenburg and countersigned by General Kurt von Schleicher, Minister of Defense. Von Schleicher later bacame the last Chancellor of the Weimar Republic, and was killed in the 1934 Röhm Purge. (Bundesarchiv — Militärarchiv)

During the First World War Ewald von Kleist formed a friendship with Crown Prince Wilhelm, eldest son of Kaiser Wilhelm II and heir to the German throne. The Crown Prince was (like von Kleist) a cavalry officer, commanding the 1. Leibhusaren-Regiment and later an Army Group on the Western Front. In 1935, Wilhelm presented this superb portrait photograph to von Kleist as a token of their friendship. It bears a handwritten inscription which has not been deciphered, but which appears to be poetic verse of a military nature. The gorget worn by the Crown Prince bears an Imperial eagle upon which is superimposed the death's-head emblem of the Hussars.

June 10, 1936. As Commanding General of the VIII. Armeekorps (Wehrkreis VIII) at Breslau, Generalleutnant von Kleist reviews a parade of Infanterie-Rgt. 28 at the Neuhammer training area. The mounted officer to his right (wearing helmet and holding sabre) is probably the Regimental Commander. (Christa von Kleist).

Gen. von Kleist confers with two of his officers during war games exercises. Note the battle practice helmet band worn by the officer immediately behind him. (Christa von Kleist)

In August 1936, von Kleist was promoted to the rank of General der Kavallerie. He is seen here (second from right) with staff officers of the VIII.A.K. at Breslau. (Christa von Kleist)

Im Namen des Reichs
ernenne ich den Generalleutnant
Ewald von Kleist
Kommandierender General des VIII. Armeekorps
mit Wirkung vom 1. August 1936 zum
General der Kavallerie
mit einem Rangdienstalter vom 1. August 1936 (1).
Jch vollziehe diese Urkunde in der Erwartung, daß der Ernannte, getreu seinem Diensteide seine Berufspflichten zum Wohle des Reichs erfüllt und das Vertrauen rechtfertigt, das ihm durch diese Ernennung bewiesen wird.
Zugleich sichere ich ihm meinen besonderen Schutz zu.
Berlin, den 2. August 1936.
Der Führer und Reichskanzler

Im Namen des Führers und Reichskanzlers
verleihe ich
dem   General der Kavallerie Ewald von Kleist
(Dienstgrad, Vor- und Zuname)
Generalkommando VIII.Armeekorps
(Truppenteil)
für 25 jährige treue Dienste in der Wehrmacht die
Dienstauszeichnung IV. bis I.   Klasse.
Berlin , den 2.Oktober   1936
Der Reichskriegsminister u.Oberbefehlshaber
der Wehrmacht
von Blomberg
Generalfeldmarschall
Für die Richtigkeit:
Jn Vertretung:
des Chefs des Generalstabes
(Dienstgrad und Dienststellung)
Major im Generalstab.

An avid hunter, Ewald von Kleist is seen here after taking a magnificent stag. The location is probably in the area of the family estate near Breslau, Silesia. It is interesting to note that several fine hunting rifles and shotguns were found carefully stored among his personal belongings in June 1945. (Christa von Kleist)

General d. Kav. von Kleist on horseback near the training area of the VIII.A.K. near Neuhammer, Silesia. (Tim Knight)

On February 28, 1938, General von Kleist was released from active duty and placed on "z.V." status (retired but available for recall). On that date Adolf Hitler presented him with this signed portrait, complete with silver frame. The handwritten inscription reads: "Herr General der Kavallerie von Kleist, with my best wishes — Adolf Hitler, Berlin on 28 Feb. 1938".

Ewald von Kleist's Badge of the Order of St. John Hospitaller of Jerusalem (Grand Priory of Brandenburg). Von Kleist became a Knight of Honor of this famous religious order in 1917 as a Hauptmann in the General Staff of the Garde-Kavallerie-Division. In 1935 has was made a Knight of Justice by the Order's Grand Master, Prinz Oskar von Preussen. (Christa von Kleist)

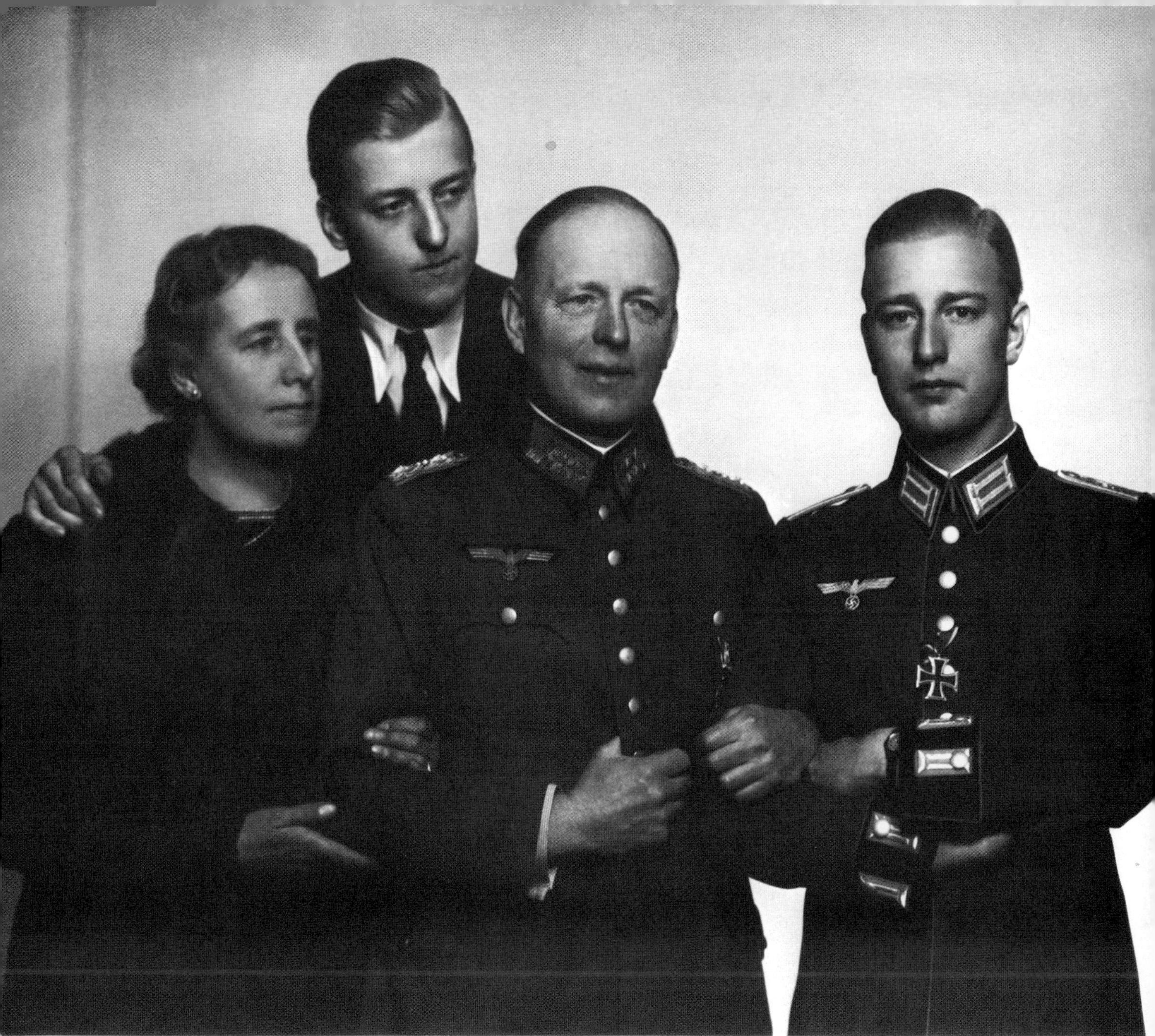

The Ewald von Kleist family. This portrait photograph was made in 1940, prior to the invasion of France. Von Kleist is seen here as General der Kavallerie, and wears the 1939 Spange to the Iron Cross 1st Class (awarded for his successes in the Polish campaign). Frau Gisela von Kleist is at his side, and son Heinrich stands behind his father and mother. Son Ewald is in uniform as a Leutnant of Cavalry and wears the Iron Cross 2nd Class (won in the Polish campaign). (Christa von Kleist)

On May 12, 1940, Panzergruppe Kleist crosses the French border from Belgium and drives on Sedan, site of the disastrous French defeat in 1870 and the surrender of Napoleon III.

Although French forces had destroyed all bridges over the River Maas, von Kleist's drive was delayed very little. Spearheaded by the 1st and 2nd Panzer Divisions under General Guderian, Panzergruppe Kleist crossed the river in force on May 14.

Generalleutnant Reinhardt, Commanding General of XLI. Korps under Panzergruppe Kleist, leads the northern fork of von Kleist's thrust through France.

General Giraud, commanding the French 7th Army, is captured by advancing German forces along with his staff only shortly after assuming his command.

Many French tanks are abandoned intact in the face of the German advance.

A German soldier displays the captured standard of the French 145th Infantry Regiment.

Captured French Army Company flags are examined by a Corporal of Panzergruppe Kleist.

French and Allied troops are captured in large numbers. Shown are French Colonial soldiers and members of the British Expeditionary Force.

The port city of Boulogne is overrun by the 2nd Panzer Division on May 23, 1940. In this photo, German troops use a captured French coastal battery to fire on a British destroyer.

A Panzer II of the Panzergruppe Kleist advances northward near the Channel Coast toward Dunkirk. By Hitler's order, the advance was halted on May 24.

The advance of German armour toward Dunkirk is resumed on the night of May 26, but too late to prevent the British evacuation across the Channel. Still, large numbers of British vehicles are abandoned during the withdrawal.

Generaloberst Walter von Brauchitsch, Commander-in-Chief of the German Army, visits the headquarters of Panzergruppe Kleist before the start of the German advance southward into the heart of France. General von Kleist is behind him in the picture (partly obscured).

General der Infanterie Gustav von Wietersheim, Commanding General of XIV. Korps, at the Amiens bridgehead over the Somme River.

The commander of a Panzer II observes the situation as his unit moves forward. The aiguillette he wears indicates that this officer is a unit adjutant.

Motorcycle troops nap during a pause in the rapid advance. The white "K" on the motorcycle headlights denote that these are units of Panzergruppe Kleist.

Using rubber rafts, German soldiers ferry equipment during the initial crossings of the Seine River on June 15.

On June 16, 1940, XVI.Korps under General der Kavallerie Erich Hoepner reaches Dijon. Here Hoepner reviews battle maps with his unit commanders. This outstanding officer was later to become involved in the July 1944 plot to assassinate Hitler, and was executed for that involvement.

General von Kleist in his staff car during the final stages of the Battle of France. Seated in the rear of the car is Oberst Kurt Zeitzler, von Kleist's Chief of Staff in France and also in Russia. He later reached the rank of Generaloberst and became Chief of the Army General Staff.

Forces of Panzergruppe Kleist in Orleans on June 20. The Orleans Cathedral is in the background.

On June 29, 1940, the spearhead of Panzergruppe Kleist under General von Wietersheim reaches the Spanish border. Von Wietersheim (together with German Army, Navy, SS, Political, & Diplomatic officers) is seen here greeting officers of the Spanish Army on the border at Irun. This event marked the completion of the geographical conquest of France.

VORWORT

Zehntausende von Kraftfahrzeugen führten in Frankreich das **K** als Erkennungszeichen ihrer Zugehörigkeit zu einer starken motorisierten Gruppe.

Das **K** erschien an der Kanalküste, an der Somme=Oise, an der Schweizer Grenze und an der Atlantischen Küste bis zu den Pyrenäen.

Das **K** kannte Freund und Feind.

Uns alle verbindet eine verwirrende Fülle der Eindrücke und Erinnerungen.

Sie zu ordnen und festzuhalten soll dieses Buch dienen.

v. Kleist
GENERALOBERST

Foreword written by von Kleist for the book "Mit dem K durch Frankreich", published in 1941 to commemorate the achievements of the Panzergruppe Kleist in the Battle of France.

General Ewald von Kleist in conversation with Adolf Hitler at the field kitchen of the Führerhauptquartier "Felsennest" during the Battle of France. Von Kleist is wearing the Knight's Cross of the Iron Cross, which was awarded to him during the opening days of the campaign. (National Archives)

Another view of von Kleist at "Felsennest". Here he is in conversation with Generaloberst Hans Gunther von Kluge, Commanding General of the 4th Army during the French campaign. Von Kluge is to the left in the picture, and behind him (partly obscured) is Martin Bormann in SS uniform. Hitler can be seen in the background between von Kluge and von Kleist. (National Archives)

General von Kleist and the staff of his Panzergruppe. Fourth from the right is Oberst Kurt Zeitzler, von Kleist's Chief of Staff. Although undated, it is believed that this photo was taken following the conclusion of the French campaign.

A Panzer band is reviewed by Gen. von Kleist. All members of the band are wearing the special black Panzer uniform.

Im Namen
des
Deutschen Volkes

befördere ich
den General der Kavallerie z.V.
Ewald von Kleist
mit sofortiger Wirkung
zum Generaloberst.

Ich vollziehe diese Urkunde in der Erwartung,
daß der Genannte getreu seinem Diensteide
seine Berufspflichten gewissenhaft erfüllt und
das Vertrauen rechtfertigt, das ihm durch
diese Beförderung bewiesen wird. Zugleich
sichere ich ihm meinen besonderen Schutz zu.

Führerhauptquartier, den 19. Juli 1940

Der Führer

Official document promoting Gen. d. Kav. von Kleist to Generaloberst effective July 19, 1940. This promotion was conferred in recognition of his exceptional performance in the French Campaign. Personally signed by Hitler, the document is contained in a red leather binder with an impressed gold national eagle on its cover. (Charles Scaglione & Robert Sevier)

Portrait of Generaloberst von Kleist, from one of a series of portrait postcards entitled "Der Führer und seine Generale des Heeres" ("The Führer and his Army Generals"), published by authority of the Army High Command (OKH).

Following the surrender of France, Hitler takes the salute of the crowd as his auto drives over a carpet of flowers in a triumphal parade through the streets of Berlin. Seated immediately behind Hitler is his personal Adjutant, SS-Gruppenführer Julius Schaub. In the rear seat is Wilhelm Keitel, Chief of the OKW. (Author's Collection)

Generalfeldmarschall Wilhelm List. List commanded the 12th Army (of which von Kleist's Panzergruppe I was a part) in the conquest of Yugoslavia. Earlier he commanded 12th Army in France and 14th Army in Poland, both of which included von Kleist's Panzers. He was later again von Kleist's commanding officer when he briefly served as Oberbefehlshaber of Army Group A in Russia from July to September 1942. (Author's Collection)

Bulgaria, March 1941. Generaloberst von Kleist and SS-Obergruppenführer Sepp Dietrich (commanding the Leibstandarte-SS "Adolf Hitler") meet prior to the invasion of Yugoslavia.

March 27, 1941. Von Kleist and King Boris of Bulgaria observe a Luftwaffe rangefinder in action during a training exercise at Samokov.

April 8, 1941. Von Kleist's Panzergruppe I begins its thrust into Yugoslavia. He is seen here with Gen. d. Inf. Gustav von Wietersheim (commanding XIV.Pz.Korps) at the Yugoslavian-Bulgarian border.

April 8, 1941. Generaloberst von Kleist observes the crossing of his forces into Yugoslavia. To the right in the photo is his Orderly Officer, Oberleutnant Harry von Johnston.

Generaloberst von Kleist in his SdKfz 251 armored command vehicle. Note the frame-type radio antenna for long-range communications with the combat units. The black Panzer Beret (Schutzmütze) is still being worn.

Panzergruppe I rapidly drives North toward the Yugoslavian capital of Belgrade. Von Kleist is seen at the extreme left in this photo during a brief pause in the advance.

Serbian soldiers of the Yugoslavian army after surrendering to the Germans.

On April 12 Belgrade falls. A German vehicle drives past the Serbian Parliament building.

An unusual snapshot of the bedroom of Generaloberst von Kleist's personal quarters in Belgrade, April 13.

April 13, 1941. Von Kleist reviews a victory parade of German forces in the streets of Belgrade. A column of Pz.III's are seen here.

In this view of the victory parade, a Pz.II passes the reviewing point.

Generalfeldmarschall Gerd von Rundstedt, Oberbefehlshaber of Army Group South in Russia until December 1941, was von Kleist's commanding officer during the initial phase of the Russian campaign. He had also commanded Army Group South in Poland and Army Group A in France, both of which included von Kleist's forces. (Author's Collection)

On June 22, 1941, Panzergruppe I crosses into Soviet territory west of Rovno. Here a column of Pz.III's advance eastward following an air strike by Stukas of Luftflotte 4.

The 11th Panzer Division is part of the spearhead of the advance into Russia. This photo gives an excellent closeup of the vehicle markings used by this division. Above the vehicle number is the division's own special emblem — a skull-faced ghost with sword in hand, standing astride a fast-moving vehicle. Because of this insignia, the 11.Pz.Div. is known by the nickname "Ghost Division". Above the divisional emblem is a large white "K" which denotes the vehicle as a part of von Kleist's Panzergruppe. Von Kleist originated the use of such a marking in the invasion of France, and vehicles of his command continued to wear the "K" through Yugoslavia and Russia.

A Pz.III of 11.Pz.Div. moves forward as the attack progresses. The "Ghost Division" emblem can be seen on the side of the tank below the turret.

A "Panzerbefehlswagen" (command vehicle) of 11.Pz.Div. crosses a Russian bridge. These "command tanks" exercised radio control over tanks in combat, serving as mobile command posts. Made on the chassis of the Pz.I, very few of these vehicles were built. The emblem appearing on the front of the vehicle below the machine gun is the "official" marking of the 11.Pz.Div.

German casualties during the early fighting. In the foreground is a PzBfw.I of the 11.Pz.Div.

A remarkable series of three sequential combat photographs. In this picture, a Pz.III has just scored a hit on a Russian tank. On the side of the Pz.III's turret is the abbreviation "Adj.", indicating that this is the tank of the unit's Adjutant (probably the Adjutant of Panzer Regiment 15 in this case).

In the next shot, crewmen of the German tank (armed with MP-40's) rush forward on foot toward the burning Russian tank. A crewman of the Russian vehicle has gotten out and is running toward the Germans with his hands up.

In the third and final shot, the German Panzer crew examines the Russian tank they have just destroyed (a T-26B).

The same Pz.III advances past a burning building. In this view, the "Adj." marking can be seen on the rear of the turret as well as on the side. On the rear of the chassis can be seen the "K" of Panzergruppe I (Kleist).

The Adjutant's tank moves on, accompanied by German infantry.

German tankers search Russian prisoners. Again, the Pz.III of the Regimental Adjutant can be seen in the background.

One more time! The unit Adjutant's Pz.III (a very popular rank with the photographer). This tank and its crew apparently also saw combat in the French campaign, since two captured French helmets decorate the front of the vehicle as "war souvenirs".

July 7, 1941, near Ostrog. Von Kleist gives orders to Sepp Dietrich concerning the attack of the Leibstandarte-SS "Adolf Hitler" against the fortified "Stalin Line".

July 9, near Ostrog. A Soviet STZ "Komsomolets" light gun tractor abondoned on the battlefield.

Another view of the battlefield near Ostrog on July 9. Russian guns and equipment litter the area.

The Russian defensive positions have been penetrated. On July 10 near Zwiahel, a German officer examines the effect of a shell hit on a pillbox of the "Stalin Line".

Despite destruction of bridges by the retreating Soviets, German troops push on across a river near Zwiahel on July 10 using rubber rafts.

July 11, 1941. Generaloberst von Kleist en route
to Zwiahel.

On the road to Zwiahel on July 11, von Kleist pauses to talk with Ukranian
civilians. Standing in the car is his translator, Prof. Dr. Wilhelm. Oberleutnant
von Johnston, his Orderly Officer, is seated in the rear.

Another view of the same scene on July 11. Ukranians for
the most part welcomed the Germans as liberators from
the oppressive Stalin regime. Note the Field Policeman
(upper left of photo), part of von Kleist's security
contingent.

On July 30, 1941, von Kleist's staff car crosses the Ross
River near Boguslav.

Still on July 30, von Kleist makes another river crossing (by means of a submerged bridge) in the region West of Kiev. Oberleutnant von Johnston is standing in the rear of the staff car.

July 30, 1941. Gen.Ob. von Kleist presents the Knight's Cross of the Iron Cross to General der Kavallerie Eberhard von Mackensen, commander of III.A.K.(mot).

On August 1, 1941, von Kleist presents the Knight's Cross to Generalmajor Düvert, commander of the 13th Panzer Divison. The location is Korsun.

Von Kleist surveys the battlefield at Boguslav on August 1.

August 1, Korsun. After the award ceremony, von Kleist and Düvert discuss battle plans for the 13.Pz.Division.

As Panzergruppe I pushes East, large numbers of Russian tanks are destroyed or abandoned. Here Generaloberst von Kleist examines a huge multi-turreted T-35 which was abandoned intact by its crew.

Another monstrous but impractical Soviet tank was the KV-2. A German soldier examines the huge turret of one of these tanks, which has been blown completely off by artillery fire.

During their retreat the Russian forces litter the field with equipment. Here horse-drawn wagons have been abandoned in a roadside ditch. A heavy tractor and an obsolete BT-5 tank are in the background.

Generalfeldmarschall Walter von Brauchitsch, Commander-in-Chief of the German Army, arrives for a visit on the front. Generaloberst von Kleist (at left) greets him at the airstrip. Von Brauchitsch was dismissed by Hitler on December 19, 1941, and his authority was assumed by Hitler himself.

After the inspection tour, von Kleist (right) and von Brauchitsch exchange a warm handshake before the Commander-in-Chief departs. These two officers were friends of many years' standing.

September 3, 1941. Generaloberst von Kleist and a senior Hungarian officer pause in the field. Von Kleist's orderly officer and his translator stand beside the car.

September 3, at Tomakavka near Zaporozhye, Generaloberst von Kleist participates in a battle conference with Hungarian General von Miklas. At this stage of the Russian campaign, Hungarian military participation was only a token involvement.

Von Kleist and senior Hungarian army officers observe the front near Zaporozhye, Sept. 3.

German tanks and infantry move across the heart of the Ukraine.

Elements of 11.Pz.Division. The ammunition trailer towed by the halftrack in the foreground bears the division's "Ghost" emblem as well as its official vehicle marking (a circle with a vertical dividing bar).

An armored command car (SdKfz 221) of 11.Pz.Div. races down a dusty road. Note the numerous radio antennae.

A Pz.III command tank uses trees and brush for camoflage.

The same command tank a few moments later. Its crew is very effectively concealing their vehicle with vegetation.

Tank crews of 11.Pz.Div. break down and clean the machine guns from their Panzers during a break in the advance.

A tank crew digs a temporary shelter under their vehicle for safety during the coming night.

General der Panzertruppe Werner Kempf, commanding XLVIII.Panzer-Korps. His forces had driven to the western bank of the Dnieper River near Kremenchug, and would play a major role in the upcoming battle of Kiev. Gen. Kempf was awarded the Knight's Cross as commander of 6.Panzer-Division in France under Panzergruppe Kleist.

Gen. Kempf and Gen.Ob. von Kleist plan the participation of Kempf's XLVIII.Pz.K. in the northward drive to encircle Kiev.

Von Kleist leaves the headquarters of XLVIII.Pz.Korps after the battle conference.

Tanks of Panzergruppe I (Kleist) move northward to encircle the city of Kiev and to link with Guderian's Panzergruppe II.

The attack moves forward toward Kiev.

SdKfz.251 Armored Personnel Carriers of Panzergruppe I advance through a Russian village.

A dead Russian soldier lies in the mud along the path of the attack. Note the white "K" on the German vehicles in the background.

A German medic (left, in black cap) assists a wounded Russian soldier after the great encirclement at Kiev. Over 660,000 Russians were taken prisoner in this battle.

Russian prisoners captured in the Kiev pocket carry a wounded comrade.

A Soviet KV-1 heavy tank burns during the battle for Kiev. Over 800 Russian armored vehicles were destroyed or captured.

Sept. 18, 1941. Generaloberst von Kleist attends a situation conference at the headquarters of XI Army Corps (an element of 11th Army). The officer in the center is Generalmajor Sachs, Commander of 257 Inf.Division.

September 18. In conversation with General der Infanterie Koch, Commanding General of XLIV Army Corps. A light flak unit mounted on the truck in the background provides anti-aircraft cover.

Sept. 27. Von Kleist boards his Fieseler Fi 156 "Storch" aircraft for a flight to Kremenchug.

An aerial view of the Ukranian countryside from von Kleist's "Storch" during the flight to Kremenchug on Sept. 27. The Russians have destroyed the bridge in the foreground. German units are crossing the river using a pontoon bridge and the intact railway bridge in the background.

At Kremenchug on the Dnieper River for an inspection tour on Sept. 27. In the background, Russian prisoners load supplies onto a German truck.

Von Kleist and Oberleutnant von Johnston observe passing units of the 16.Panzer-Div. near Zaritschanka on Sept. 28. The halftrack in the foreground tows an 8.8 cm flak gun.

Oberst d.R. Hyazinth Graf Strachwitz. As a Major commanding I./Pz.Rgt.2 of the 16.Pz.Divison, Strachwitz was awarded the Knight's Cross on August 25, 1941 during the drive through the Ukraine. A brilliant tank officer, he later achieved the rank of Generalmajor and became one of only 27 men to be awarded the Knight's Cross with Oakleaves, Swords, and Diamonds. (Author's Collection)

Sept. 28, 1941, near Zaritschanka. Gen.Ob. von Kleist briefs an Italian General and his staff on the situation.

Von Kleist at Zaritschanka on Sept. 28, in conversation with Gen.Maj. Düvert (Commander of 13.Pz.Div.) and Generalarbeitsführer Dr. Schmeidler of the RAD.

Awarding the Iron Cross to officers and men of the RAD (Reich Labor Service). RAD personnel performed construction and other duties on the Russian Front, often under combat conditions.

Von Kleist steps from his staff car in the square of an unidentified city in the southern Ukraine. On the front fenders of his car can be seen his Command Flag as "Befehlshaber einer Panzergruppe" and the vehicle pennant for an Army General.

Situation conference in the town square with an unidentified Generalmajor, using the staff car's hood as a table.

October 4, 1941. Panzergruppe I has established bridgeheads on the Dnieper River at Dnepropetrovsk and Zaporozhye. In this photo, Gen.Ob. von Kleist surveys damage to a major Russian bridge near Dnepropetrovsk.

On October 4 at Dnepropetrovsk, von Kleist conducts a situation conference with General Messe, commander of Italian forces in the Ukraine. Messe was later transferred to North Africa, and was promoted to Field Marshal on May 13, 1943; he surrendered on the day of his promotion.

Von Kleist and Messe leaving after their conference. Both seem to be amused at the appearance of the Italian guard in the foreground.

Von Kleist and Oberst Zeitzler visit the great Dnieper dam and hydroelectric power station at Zaporozhye, captured intact by Panzergruppe I. The dam was constructed for Russia by American engineers.

Zaporozhye, October 9. An inspection tour of a foundry destroyed by the retreating Soviets.

Oct. 16, 1941, a training ship in the harbor at Mariupol on the Sea of Azov.

Von Kleist, Oberst Zeitzler, and staff officers aboard the training ship at Mariupol.

A sunken Russian vessel in the harbor at Mariupol, October 16.

October 18, 1941, at Mariupol. Von Kleist tours a munitions factory which had manufactured bombs for the Red air force. In the center of the photo, his personal translator is in conversation with an official of the factory.

Von Kleist in conversation with an unidentified Rumanian General (possibly the commander of the Rumanian 4th Army) on October 18 at Mariupol.

October 27, 1941. A visit to an iron foundry at Mariupol, the largest in the Ukraine.

Mariupol, October 27. Von Kleist visits a Luftwaffe reconnaissance squadron. The aircraft is an Me-110 Zerstorer twin-engine fighter, converted for long-range reconnaissance use.

The operation of the aerial reconnaissance camera is explained to von Kleist. The Luftwaffe officer in the center is the Staffel Commander, Hauptmann Schäfer. Schäfer wears the Spanish Cross with Swords, indicating that he flew in combat with the Legion Condor in Spain.

From late October thru mid-November, 1941, the autumn mud halted all operations along the Eastern Front, including those of von Kleist's command (which had been upgraded in October from Panzergruppe to First Panzer Army).

On November 15, shortly before the resumption of the eastward advance, von Kleist pays a visit to the SS-Division Leibstandarte-SS "Adolf Hitler" east of the Mius River. To the right is the Division commander, SS-Obergruppenführer Dietrich. The officer in the center is SS-Sturmbannführer Georg Schonberger, who was awarded the Knight's Cross posthumously after being killed in action Nov. 20, 1943.

The Commander-in-Chief of I.Panzerarmee enjoys a schnapps with the officers of the "Adolf Hitler" Division, November 15, 1941.

Von Kleist converses with men of the LSSAH. Some of the SS soldiers are wearing captured Russian winter clothing.

Generalfeldmarschall Walter von Reichenau, Commander-in-Chief of Army Group South from December 1, 1941 until his sudden death on January 17, 1942 as the result of a stroke. During the brief period of his command, the Russian army mounted a winter offensive and temporarily recaptured the city of Rostov (Author's Collection).

With Gen. d. Kav. von Mackensen during the winter of 1941-42. Von Mackensen, Commander of III.Pz.Korps, wears a heavy Russian fur cap.

A candid photo of Generaloberst von Kleist during the Russian winter.

Von Kleist and an unidentified Panzer Oberst snack on eggs.

At the airfield at Stalino on February 17, 1942. Stalino has been in German hands since October 20, 1941. The lingering cold of the Russian winter is evidenced by the heavy clothing worn by von Kleist and the officer in the background.

In February 1942, Generaloberst von Kleist receives the Oakleaves to his Knight's Cross. The award is presented personally by Adolf Hitler, in recognition of von Kleist's outstanding leadership during the conquest of the Ukraine.

A badly-lighted but striking candid photograph of Generaloberst Ewald von Kleist, probably taken shortly after his decoration with the Oakleaves to his Knight's Cross of the Iron Cross.

With Generalfeldmarschall Fedor von Bock in the spring of 1942. Von Bock had been appointed Commander-in-Chief of Army Group South in January 1942, following the death of GFM von Reichenau, and he held that post until his dismissal by Hitler in July. The location is probably von Bock's headquarters at Poltava.

On the morning of May 17, 1942, von Kleist's I.Panzerarmee and 17.Armee (temporarily united as "Army Group Kleist") mount an attack northward to execute "Operation Fridericus" — the encirclement of the massive Soviet forces south of Kharkov.

Panzers of Armeegruppe Kleist advance toward Kharkov along a Russian rail line.

Another truly remarkable series of sequential combat photographs. In this first view, advancing German forces have caught Russian aircraft on the ground on a makeshift airfield. A 20mm flak gun mounted on a halftrack opens fire on a nearby Russian fighter, and the camera catches the shell at the moment of impact.

As the first fighter burns, the gun turns and fires on a second aircraft. It has just fired, and the shell is still in flight to the target.

In the third and final photo, the gun has fired again on a third Russian aircraft (apparently a small bomber). Again the camera catches the shell at the moment of impact, and the shell's smoke trail from gun to target can be seen.

German artillery fires on the enemy.

As the battle progresses, German Infantry observe burning buildings from high ground.

An 8.8cm flak gun, used as an anti-tank weapon, fires on advancing Soviet armour.

A Russian tank has exploded after a German shell hit its ammo magazine. Totally destroyed, the tank is unrecognizable as to type.

Another Russian tank — this time a BT-7 — burns. A direct hit has blown the turret completely off.

German infantry rushes forward under fire.

An SdKfz 10 halftrack mounting an anti-tank gun advances. German infantry move through the field in the background.

Russian dead on the battlefield south of Kharkov.

Russian dead, plus their horses and equipment, litter the roadside as an SdKfz 6/2 halftrack with flak gun passes in the background.

More Russian casualties of the massive German attack.

Huge quantities of Russian equipment are abandoned as the German forces complete the encirclement. Here several artillery pieces are examined by German soldiers.

A Russian T-26 B tank and a howitzer are only a tiny part of the equipment captured in the pocket south of Kharkov.

Von Kleist in his Fieseler "Storch" prior to takeoff. The interesting emblem on the plane appears to be that of a figure riding on a winged unicycle while looking through a telescope.

The great battle concluded, Gen.Ob. von Kleist and his personal pilot prepare to take off for an inspection of the battlefield from the air.

An aerial view of the battlefield south of Kharkov, taken by aricraft of Luftwaffe Aufklärungsgruppe 4/32. Just left of center is a knocked-out T-34 tank. Immediately in front of the T-34 is an over-turned ambulance.

Horse-drawn supply wagons and dead horses litter the field.

A totally destroyed Russian troop train. The original photo caption reads, "Direct hit by Stukas".

An enormous column of captured Russian soldiers in the pocket south of Kharkov. In this great battle over 230,000 Soviet Army prisoners were taken, and some 1,500 tanks and 2,000 guns were destroyed or captured by von Kleist's forces.

Generaloberst Ewald von Kleist and General d. Kavallerie Eberhard von Mackensen following the German victory south of Kharkov. Von Mackensen, whose III.Pz.Korps had played a key role in "Operation Fridericus", was awarded the Oakleaves to his Knight's Cross for the achievements of his command. He is wearing the Oakleaves in this photo.

Von Kleist's mobile quarters and command trailer at Pavlograd, east of Dnepropetrovsk, in June 1942.

Temporary headquarters of I.Panzerarmee at Pavlograd, June 1942.

Following the great battle south of Kharkov, the Panzers resume their eastward drive.

A Panzer column of I.Panzerarmee moves East.

During a pause in the advance, a motorcycle driver takes a welcome rest. The turret of a Pz.III protrudes above the grass in the background.

On June 30, 1942, Generaloberst Erich von Manstein was promoted to Generalfeldmarschall for his conquest of the Crimea. In February 1943 he was appointed Commander-in-Chief of Army Group South. Unquestionably a superb commander and perhaps the German Army's finest strategist, von Manstein and von Kleist worked closely together during the defensive battles and German retreats in southern Russia in 1943-44. He is seen here receiving his Field Marshal's baton at Hitler's "Werwolf" field headquarters in the Ukraine. The cases on the table in the foreground contain the full-dress Marshal's baton (shorter case) and the "swagger stick" baton for daily use. (National Archives)

Alfred Rosenberg, Reich Minister for the Occupied Eastern Territories, greets a contingent of the many thousands of Russians who volunteered to fight in German uniform against the oppressive Soviet regime of Josef Stalin. Rosenberg was a weak figurehead leader who could not even control his own subordinates — especially the fanatical Gauleiter Erich Koch, Reichskommissar for the Ukraine. Koch's policies in the Ukraine, as harsh as Stalin's, failed to cultivate the basic anti-communist sentiments of the populace. Such policies caused endless troubles for the military forces of von Kleist and other commanders in the occupied areas, and contributed in no small part to the German defeat in the East. (Peter G. Bilheimer/Hoover Library)

Soviet partisans surrender to I. Panzerarmee.

Another view of the captured partisans. Such "guerilla" fighters were a constant thorn in the side of the Germans in Russia.

A dead partisan, killed in a hit-and-run attack on advancing German troops.

July 10, 1942, near Lissitschansk. The great summer offensive is under way. The original caption to this photo reads: "African sand — in the Ukraine". The area is the Donez Basin above Rostov.

A comic sign errected on the roadside near Stalino, July 11. The sign directs vehicle operators to the 196th Repair Company for needed maintenance work.

A Panzer column on the move at twilight near Lissitschansk on July 12, 1942. The caption reads: "Evening falls — our tanks roll onward".

July 12, near Lissitschansk. Once again, large numbers of prisoners are taken in the German offensive. Two destroyed T-34 tanks are in the foreground.

Another view on July 12, 1942. The caption reads: "Rearward flow of Russian prisoners backs up to the Donez River". Note the destroyed T-34.

Russian prisoners await removal to the rear.

Civilians passing down a road observe captured Russian soldiers. A Pz.III stands by, as other tanks advance in the background.

German Panzer men prepare to place a seriously wounded Russian soldier in a waiting ambulance.

German soldiers examine the wreckage of a downed Soviet aircraft, mangled beyond recognition.

On July 13, 1942, the first German Infantry units cross the Donez at Ustinovka using rubber rafts.

A motorcycle is loaded on a rubber raft for the crossing of the Donez at Ustinovka on July 13.

July 13, 1942. An SdKfz 223 armored command car is ferried across the Donez by raft.

German engineers work to erect a bridge across the Donez at Ustinovka on July 13.

Infantry advances through the town of Pereschtschepnaja on July 13, 1942, after crossing the Donez River.

A Russian woman gives cold water to German soldiers at Pereschtschepnaja on July 13. Again, the Germans are a welcome sight to local civilians.

Infantry moves up carefully along a heavily-mined road near Nischneje on July 13, 1942.

In a field near Nischneje on July 13, soldiers probe carefully with their bayonets for Russian mines.

Wooden mines are removed from the ground and made harmless.

On July 17, a column of Panzer III's prepares to cross the Donez River at Lissitschansk.

Panzers cross the Donez bridgehead at Lissitschansk on July 17. This pontoon bridge was erected in one night by German Engineers.

July 19, at Alexejevka. The caption reads: "East of the Donez, on difficult Soviet roads".

Forward elements of a Jäger Division on the Don Steppe at Alexejevka.

History in a photograph. East of Novotscherkask on July 31, 1942, German troops cross the dam over the Manyisch River from Europe into Asia.

July 31, east of Novotscherkask. German soldier on a camel. The German Army is now fighting on Asian soil.

A light flak gun guards the Manyisch bridgehead against air attack, July 31.

German forces crossing the Manyisch bridgehead. In this picture, horse-drawn wagons are being used to carry supplies.

On August 1, 1942, Generaloberst von Kleist crosses the Don River at Rostov. Note the command flag for Commander-in-Chief of an Army on the rear of the near vehicle. Von Kleist himself rides in an open staff car two cars in front of this one.

Von Kleist on the Kuban Steppe of the Caucasus on August 1. This picture gives an exceptional view of the command flag on the car's left front fender, and a metal plate with the same design above the bumper. The white "K" can also be seen on the left fender, as well as the letters "WH" (for "Wehrmacht-Heer").

Civilians worship in a Russian Orthodox church at Novotscherkask on August 1, 1942. The original caption reads: "After long years of religious oppression, German entry reopens the churches".

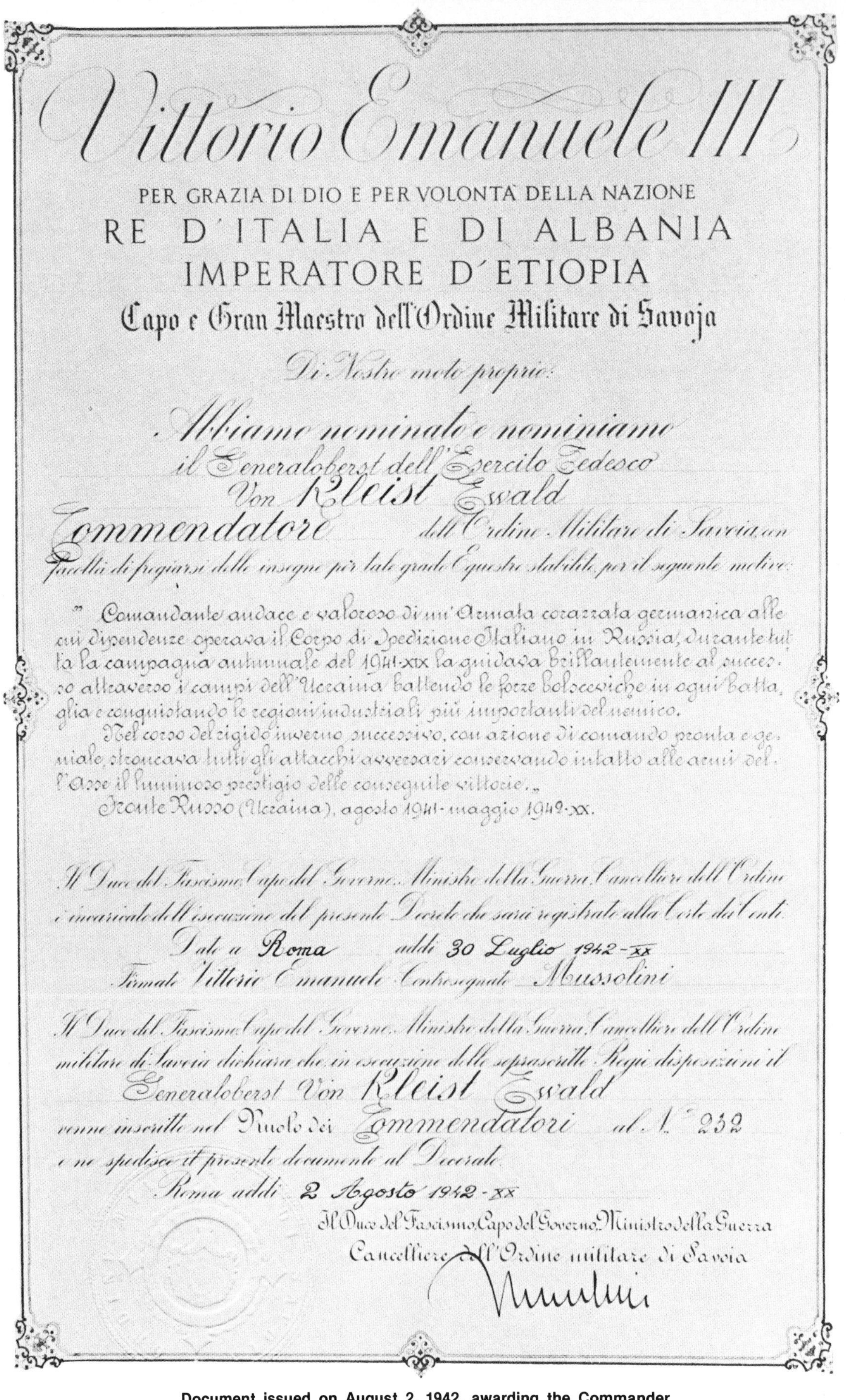

Document issued on August 2, 1942, awarding the Commander Class of the Italian Military Order of Savoy to Generaloberst von Kleist effective July 30, 1942. This award was given in recognition of his leadership of the Italian Expeditionary Corps in the Ukraine during the Fall of 1941. The Italian Expeditionary Corps was under the operational command of von Kleist. This award document is personally signed by Mussolini. (Charles Scaglione & Robert Sevier)

Generaloberst von Kleist, Oberbefehlshaber I.Panzer-armee, on August 8, 1942.

Von Kleist and his Orderly Officer, Harry von Johnston, on August 8. Von Kleist wears the Army officer's old-style white summer uniform tunic with stand-up collar. The occassion was his 61st birthday.

Crossing the Kuban River on August 10, 1942. This picture affords another excellent view of the Command Flag and also the vehicle pennant for an Army general.

Von Kleist pauses to play with Russian children on the porch of a farmhouse, August 10.

Original shoulder boards worn by Generaloberst von Kleist on his field service uniform tunic in Russia up until his promotion to Field Marshal. The numeral "8" denotes his honorary connection with the 8th Cavalry Regiment during his 1938-1939 retirement. It is especially interesting to note that these shoulder boards have a golden-yellow colored underlay (denoting Cavalry) rather than the standard red underlay prescribed for Army Generals. (Christa von Kleist)

Another view of the same scene. In this picture it can be seen that Generaloberst von Kleist is wearing the metal numeral "8" on his shoulder boards. This is a holdover from his brief period of retirement from active duty in 1938-39, during which time he was accorded the special honor of wearing the uniform of Kavallerie-Regiment 8.

A Renault weapons tractor (similar to the British "Bren Gun Carrier"), captured in France in 1940, in use with the German forces in Russia in 1942. Von Kleist appears in the photo (second from left), along with an unidentified Generalleutnant.

Into the mountains of the Caucasus. German Mountain Troops on the ascent to the Elbrus Pass, August 17, 1942, near Chursuk.

Mountain Troops on the move to the Elbrus Pass on August 17.

Another view of the ascent.

The soldiers move upward toward the snow-covered slopes of the Elbrus Pass.

Mount Elbrus, elevation 18,480 ft. — the highest mountain of the Caucasus.

An aerial view of Mt. Elbrus from a German aircraft. On August 21, 1942, mountaineers of the German 1st and 4th Mountain Division climbed this magnificent mountain and planted the Reich War Flag at its peak.

August 17. Mountain Troops assult the Nachar Pass.

A pause on the ascent to the Nachar Pass.

Mountain Troops on the Nachar Pass observe Russian positions.

Temporary quarters used by von Kleist during the German drive deep into the Caucasus. His personal trailer is concealed in the trees to the right, and a sentry stands guard at left.

A magnificent aerial view of the Caucasus mountains south of Pyatigorsk.

August 26, 1942, at Shelesnovodsk near Pyatigorsk, in the southern Caucasus. This magnificent building is used by von Kleist as his headquarters until January 1943, when Soviet counteroffensives begin to drive the Germans back. Pyatigorsk was first taken by the German 3.Pz.Div. on August 10, 1942.

Another view of von Kleist's quarters at Shelesnovodsk. Harry von Johnston stands on the building's side porch.

August 26, Shelesnovodsk. A view of the mountains from von Kleist's quarters.

The Russian oil pipeline between Groznyy and Rostov, near Mineralnyye Vody. This area was taken by 23.Pz.Div. of XL.Pz.Korps under I.Panzerarmee. The oil fields at Groznyy were a prime objective of the German drive through the Caucasus, but they were never reached. In this photo, German personnel have drilled a hole in the pipeline and light oil or gasoline is spurting out under pressure. Although probably taken in August 1942, this photograph was given as a special presentation to von Kleist on July 27, 1943 — long after the German forces had been driven back from the region — by an unidentified officer. A handwritten inscription on the reverse reads: "To Generalfeldmarschall v. Kleist, in remembrance of the drilling of the Groznyy-Rostov oil pipeline near Mineralnyye Vody in the North Caucasus".

August 28, 1942, at Abdul Gazy. German soldiers with "Caucasian grapes and eggs".

August 28 at Abdul Gazy. A German war photographer films a Tartar shephered on the Kalmuk Steppe.

The war photographer films residents of a Tartar village on the Kalmuk Steppe at the edge of the Caucasian mountains.

Abdul Gazy, Aug. 28. The caption reads: "Pictures from Germany generate amazement among Tartar villagers."

A Tartar man and child at Abdul Gazy.

August 28. Tartar villagers at Abdul Gazy examine a German Army vehicle with considerable interest.

A camel-drawn wagon of nomads on the Kalmuk Steppe in the northeast Caucasus.

The Terek River. Reached by I.Panzerarmee in August 1942, the Terek marked the final limit of the German advance in the Caucasus.

Cossack squadron in the Caucasus. Thousands of Cossacks and other Russian subjects joined forces with the Germans to fight against the Soviet regime.

Armored Infantry of I.Panzerarmee in the Caucasus.

Another superb view of the twin peaks of Mt. Elbrus, as seen from Pyatigorsk in September 1942.

October 25, 1942, at Kon Sovot by Kisslovodsk. Army Stud-Farm of the I.Panzer-Armee. During the fast German advance through the Caucasus, a Soviet military stud-farm for thoroughbred horses at Kon Sovot was overrun. Most of the horses were released into the countryside. The Veterinary General of I.Panzer-armee quickly reopened the farm and organized a roundup of some 1700 thoroughbreds for use by the German Army.

German soldiers and Cossacks conduct the roundup of the Russian horses at Kon Sovot on October 25.

Von Kleist's staff at Shelesnovodsk, Christmas 1942. On November 22, 1942, Generaloberst von Kleist had been promoted to Commander-in-Chief of Army Group A, giving him command of all German ground forces in the Caucasus and later in the Crimea.

In late 1942, Gen.Ob. von Kleist gives an address to a formation of RAD (Reich Labor Service) personnel at Shelesnovodsk in the southern Caucasus. The RAD played a continuing key roll in construction and labor activities on the Russian Front, frequently at the front line itself.

A view of the parade area during von Kleist's address to the RAD.

At the conclusion of his address, von Kleist salutes the men of the RAD formation.

Von Kleist inspects the formation following his speech.

RAD units parade past the RAD headquarters building at Shelesnovodsk. Von Kleist and senior officers of the Army and RAD review the parade from the steps of the headquarters.

Generaloberst von Kleist converses with RAD Generalarbeitsführer Roch, commander of the RAD units serving with the German Army in the southern Caucasus.

In early 1943, the Russian counteroffensive in the Caucasus and northward along the Stalingrad Front begins to push the German Army back. By mid-February von Kleist's Heeresgruppe A had been forced back to the Taman peninsula. In this photo, a German gun crew unlimbers an 8.8cm flak gun in the face of advancing enemy forces.

The gun crew fires at close range on Russian tanks. The 8.8cm flak gun was one of the most famous weapons of World War II, and was probably the most effective German weapon against enemy tanks.

A soviet T-34 tank is examined by German soldiers after being destroyed by fire from an 8.8cm gun. The T-34 was a superb tank and was always a severe test for the German Panzers.

During the German retreat, a bridge is prepared for destruction in an effort to slow the Russian advance. German Army Engineers are attaching explosives to the underside of this bridge at the far end.

A knocked-out Russian T-34 tank is used by German troops as a sheltered campsite. Destroyed armour was commonly used to provide Infantry with added protection along the front lines. (Author's Collection)

A heavy gun in the Crimea, 1943.

On February 1, 1943, Ewald von Kleist was promoted to the rank of Field Marshal, highest rank in the German Army. He is seen here in attendance at a battle conference with Hitler on March 9, 1943 at the headquarters of Army Group South at Zaporozhye. The topic of discussion was, of course, German efforts to stem the heavy reversals in South Russia. Shown standing at the conference table (left to right) are Generaloberst Ruoff (17th Army), Hitler, General d. Inf. Zeitzler (Chief of the Army General Staff, and formerly Chief of Staff of von Kleist's Panzergruppe), von Kleist, and General d. Pz.Tp. Kempf (behind Kleist). The other two officers at the table are unidentified.

Another view of the battle conference with Hitler on March 9. Generalfeldmarschall von Manstein (Army Group South) is at the far left, and GFM von Kleist (Army Group A) is at the extreme right. Gen.Ob. Ruoff is briefing Hitler.

On April 15, 1943, two months after his promotion to Generalfeldmarschall, von Kleist is presented with his Marshal's baton by Hitler at the Berghof. In this photo, the magnificent baton can be seen in its open case on the piano between von Kleist and Hitler. The baton is understood to now be in an East German museum. (National Archives).

Marshal Antonescu, Rumanian Chief of State, arrives in the Crimea in 1943 for an inspection of Rumanian forces there. He is greeted at the airfield by Generalfeldmarschall von Kleist. Antonescu's personal aircraft is a German Ju 52 with Rumanian markings.

Antonescu is saluted by a Rumanian officer as von Kleist stands by.

Marshal Antonescu and GFM von Kleist prepare to depart in a staff car for the inspection tour. Antonescu is wearing the German Knight's Cross of the Iron Cross (awarded in August 1941) and the Pilot-Observer Badge in Gold with Diamonds. Von Kleist wears two classes of the Rumanian Order of Michael the Brave.

Following the inspection, Antonescu and von Kleist review an honor guard at the airfield before Antonescu departs. Von Kleist salutes the honor guard with his "swagger stick" Marshal's baton.

Antonescu and von Kleist have a final conversation before parting. A Rumanian military cameraman films the scene. This entire sequence of photos was taken by Rumanian photographers and later presented to von Kleist. As a note of interest, Antonescu was deposed by King Michael in August 1944, and was hung as a "war criminal" in June 1946.

GFM von Kleist makes an inspection of the "cable railway" facility at Kertsch, circa June 1943. This "cable railway" connected the Kertsch Peninsula (the eastern tip of the Crimea) with the Taman Peninsula on the northwestern edge of the Caucasus. Its purpose was to carry iron ore and other raw materials across the Strait of Kertsch (a narrow waterway between the Sea of Azov and the Black Sea).

During the inspection tour, an officer of the "Organisation Todt" (a non-military engineering & construction formation) briefs GFM von Kleist on the operation of the "cable railway". The officer at the extreme left is Generalmajor Förster (not further identified).

The originating terminal building of the "cable railway" at Kertsch. An inscription on the wall of the building states that the facility was constructed by Organisation Todt (OT) Troops 645 & 646 during the period of March 26 — June 2, 1943.

Ore is loaded onto a truck at Kertsch after being carried across from the Taman Peninsula on the "cable railway", which stretched a distance of 7 kilometers across the water.

A light flak gun of the Luftwaffe guards the facilities at Kertsch from Soviet air attack. The cable line can be seen stretching out to sea in the background.

GFM von Kleist arrives at the military airfield at Stade in North Germany (near Hamburg), date unknown. He is probably on a brief home leave from the front. The civilian in the dark suit (standing behind von Kleist) is Karl Schwering, von Kleist's brother-in-law. The young man at the far right is the Field Marshal's son Heinrich, an Army Sonderführer (civilian Specialist).

Von Kleist in conversation with an unidentified Luftwaffe officer at the Stade airfield.

Von Kleist with an unidentifiable General in the Crimea, 1943.
(Christa von Kleist)

GFM Ewald von Kleist, Commander-in-Chief of Army Group A, at
Simferopol in the Crimea, Autumn 1943. (Christa von Kleist)

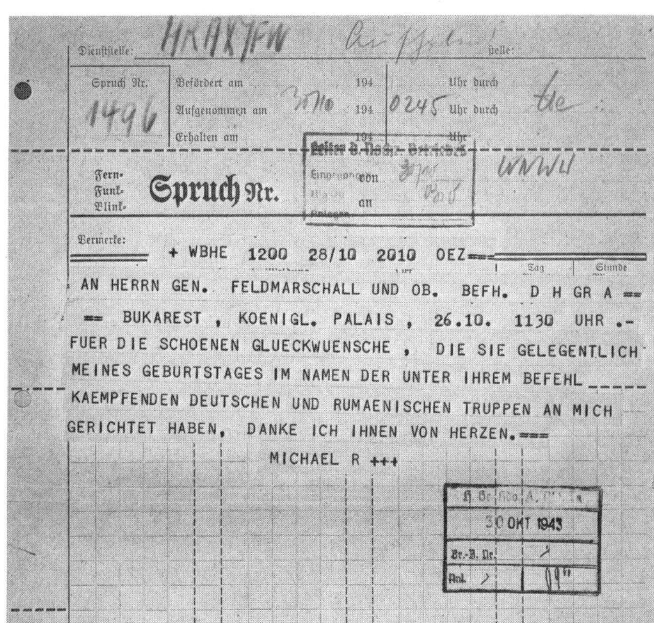

Telegram sent to Field Marshal von Kleist on October 28, 1943 by
King Michael of Rumania, thanking him for congratulatory
greetings von Kleist had sent to the King on his birthday in the
name of the German and Rumanian troops fighting under von
Kleist's command. At this time Rumanian forces were serving
under von Kleist in both the Ukraine and the Crimea.

GFM von Kleist with General der Gebirgstruppe Rudolf
Konrad (Commander of the 49th Mountain Corps) in the
Crimea, early 1944.

GFM von Kleist and Gen. Konrad observe German defensive positions at the Perekop isthmus on the northern front of the Crimea. These positions held until overwhelmed by a massive Soviet attack in early April 1944.

Generalleutnant Helmuth von Pannwitz (shown here as an Oberst in Dec. 1942). With the backing of von Kleist and Gen. Zeitzler (Army Chief of Staff), von Pannwitz was authorized to form a Cossack Division using the numerous Cossacks of the Don, Kuban, and Terek areas of southern Russia who desired to fight against communism. His Cossack forces grew rapidly in size, and in February 1945 he commanded a Cossack Cavalry Corps. At the end of the war, von Pannwitz and his Cossacks fought their way to British-held territory and surrendered to the British forces. They were promptly turned over to the Red Army, and the Cossacks were later executed almost to the man by the Soviet regime. Gen. von Pannwitz himself was hung by the Russians in January 1947. (Author's Collection)

In early 1944, GFM von Kleist pays a visit to von Pannwitz and the First Cossack Division in Croatia, where they were fighting Tito's partisans. In this scene he is awarding German decorations to men of the division. The poor quality of this and the next photograph is due to the fact that they were made from 16mm motion picture film footage. (National Archives)

Another view of GFM von Kleist decorating men of the First Cossack Division in Croatia, 1944. In the motion picture footage from which this scene was taken, the Cossacks conduct a mock cavalry charge with sabers while von Kleist observes the charge on horseback. (National Archives)

The Pz.V "Panther" tank was one of the finest tanks of World War II. Produced as Germany's answer to the Russian T-34, it was more than a match for its opponents but was available in too few numbers to turn the tide. This Panther has taken a concealed position behind vegetation along a roadway. (Author's Collection)

A "Hummel" 150 mm heavy self-propelled howitzer, seen during the German retreats in 1944. (Author's Collection)

On March 30, 1944, Adolf Hitler relieved GFM von Kleist and GFM von Manstein from their commands and placed both officers on inactive duty status. At the same time, both von Kleist and von Manstein were awarded the Swords to their Knight's Cross of the Iron Cross. Taken shortly after his removal from active duty, this is one of only two known photographs showing GFM von Kleist wearing the Swords decoration. (Christa von Kleist)

The crew of a Pz.VI "Tiger I" prepare for action in the Ukraine in early 1944. This 56-ton machine and its later brother, the Tiger II, were the ultimate in German tanks. In sufficient quantities it is very possible that the Tigers could have changed the course of the war in Russia. Only about 1350 Tiger I's and about 480 Tiger II's were ever built — far too little, too late. (Author's Collection)

A Jagdpanzer Tiger (P) "Elefant" tank destroyer, built on a Porsche Tiger chassis, on the Russian Front in 1944. Weighing 68 tons, only about 90 of these deadly tank hunters were built. The original caption of this photo reveals that it was taken on May 25, 1944 in the southern sector of the Russian Front by a War Photographer of Propaganda-Kompanie 691. (Author's Collection)

A Sturmgeschütz IV assault gun (built on a Panzer IV chassis) is held up on a Russian road in 1944 by a damaged bridge. The first Sturmgeschütz across the bridge caused extensive damage due to its weight, and Infantrymen are attempting to make repairs so the next vehicle can cross. These vehicles were excellent anti-tank weapons, and were often used by Panzer units as a substitute for tanks from 1943 onward. (Author's Collection)

March 1944 — a Sturmgeschütz III (built on the Panzer III chassis) in a Russian forest. (Author's Collection)

BESITZZEUGNIS

IM NAMEN DES FÜHRERS

WURDE DEM

Unteroffizier Christian Schlotterbeck
8./Art.Rgt.85

DER

KUBANSCHILD

VERLIEHEN

Im Felde , DEN 15. APRIL 1944

GENERALFELDMARSCHALL

Award document for the Kuban Shield decoration, presented to an NCO of the 101st Jäger Division on April 15, 1944. This document was rubber-stamp signed by GFM von Kleist and awarded to the recipient after von Kleist's release from active military duty. Instituted by Hitler in September 1943, the Kuban Shield commemorated the defensive battles of Army Group A at the Kuban bridgehead in the western Caucasus. As Commander-in-Chief of Army Group A during these battles, von Kleist was the officer designated to issue this award, and he carried out this duty even though relieved of his command.

Rubber "signature" stamp used by GFM von Kleist to sign official documents during the late war years.

Von Kleist in civilian clothes at Bad Kissingen in June 1944, three months after being relieved of his command. (Christa von Kleist)

Johannes Jürgen Christoph Ewald von Kleist, first son of GFM von Kleist. Born July 6, 1917 at Hannover, he served as a cavalry officer with the German Army and held the rank of Rittmeister at war's end. Captured by the Russians, he was held as a prisoner of war for 11 years. Ewald von Kleist died on August 8, 1976 in West Germany. (Christa von Kleist)

Hugo Edmund Christoph Heinrich von Kleist, younger son of GFM von Kleist. Born March 22, 1921 at Hannover, he served aș a Sonderführer with the German Army in Russia and was a specialist in agriculture. A severe asthma condition rendered him medically unqualified for combat duty. Heinrich von Kleist died in West Germany on March 28, 1973.

Weidebrück über Breslau, the von Kleist family estate in Silesia. Frau von Kleist and her sons can be seen in this picture. In February 1945, as the Red Army closed in on Breslau, GFM von Kleist's son Ewald blew up the manor house with high explosives to prevent its falling into Russian hands. This area is now a part of Communist Poland.

On April 25, 1945, Generalfeldmarschall von Kleist is taken into custody by the U.S. 26th Infantry Division at Mitterfels near Krenzkirchen in Lower Bavaria. The von Kleist family had evacuated from Silesia due to the Russian advance, and were living temporarily at Mitterfels along with numerous other refugees. The German officer standing beside von Kleist in this photo is Generalleutnant Russwurm, Inspector of Signal Troops. (U.S. Army Photograph)

Subsequent to his capture, GFM von Kleist was held along with other senior German officers at the Trent Park P.O.W. Camp in England. He was turned over to the Yugoslavians for trial as a "war criminal" in 1946, and was sentenced to 15 years in prison. He died on October 15, 1954, in a Russian prison camp at Wladimir in the Soviet Union. This is his official "mug shot" photograph taken upon his arrival at Trent Park in England. It is the last known photograph of Ewald von Kleist. The original photo caption reads: "General Field Marshal E. von Kleist, captured Mitterfels, Germany, 25.4.45. Held at No. 11 P.O.W. Camp Island Farm, Bridgen. Glamorgan, South Wales. Finally handed over to the Yugoslavs for trial 31.8.46." (John R. Angolia)

The official death certificate of GFM Ewald von Kleist, issued by the Soviet government on October 26, 1954. This certificate states that von Kleist died at Wladimir in the USSR on October 15, 1954 at the age of 73. The cause of death is stated as "general arteriosclerosis and hypertension". Ewald von Kleist was the only German Field Marshal to die in Russian custody. The death certificate was forwarded to his widow via the East German Ministry of Foreign Affairs. Also shown here is the transmittal letter (dated January 14, 1955) which accompanied the certificate. (Christa von Kleist)

FOOTNOTE REFERENCES

("Ref. No." citations refer to the corresponding numbered sources in the Bibliography.)

1. Ref. No. 26, p. 51.
2. Ref. No. 25, p. 73.
3. Ref. No. 26, p. 51.
4. Original document in Bundesarchiv-Militärarchiv Freiburg.
5. Original document in Bundesarchiv-Militärarchiv Freiburg.
6. Ref. No. 25, p. 74.
7. "Militärische Laufbahn" of GFM von Kleist, provided by Christa von Kleist.
8. Original document in Bundesarchiv-Militärarchiv Freiburg.
9. Ref. No. 26, p. 51.
10. Ref. No. 26, p. 51.
11. "Militärische Laufbahn" of GFM von Kleist, provided by Christa von Kleist.
12. Ref. No. 25, p. 74.
13. Ref. No. 25, p. 74.
14. Ref. No. 34, p. 22.
15. "Militärische Laufbahn" of GFM von Kleist, provided by Christa von Kleist.
16. Ref. No. 26, p. 52.
17. Ref. No. 34, p. 375.
18. Original document in Bundesarchiv-Militärarchiv Freiburg.
19. Ref. No. 22, p. 10.
20. Ref. No. 16, pp. 106-107.
21. Ref. No. 9, p. 824.
22. Ref. No. 16, p. 107.
23. Ref. No. 34. p. 398.
24. Original etching (author's collection).
25. Ref. No. 34. p. 170.
26. Original photograph (author's collection).
27. Ref. No. 7, p. 426.
28. Ref. No. 27, p. 20 (Appendix).
29. Ref. No. 34, p. 315.
30. Ref. No. 34, p. 337.
31. Ref. No. 24; also "Tagesbefehl" of the Gruppe von Kleist for June 4, 1940.
32. Ref. No. 18, p. 124.
33. Ref. No. 14, pp. 124-125.
34. Ref. No. 14, pp. 126-128.
35. Ref. No. 22, p. 91.
36. Ref. No. 14, p. 130.
37. Ref. No. 14, p. 133.
38. Ref. No. 27, p. 21 (Appendix).
39. Ref. No. 25, p. 78.
40. Original document in Bundesarchiv-Militärarchiv Freiburg.
41. Ref. No. 14, pp. 173-174.
42. Ref. No. 14, p. 175.
43. Ref. No. 14, p. 175.
44. Ref. No. 4, p. 487.
45. Original award document formerly in the possession of Charles Scaglione and Robert Sevier.
46. Ref. No. 14, pp. 201-202.
47. Ref. No. 14, p. 203.
48. Ref. No. 35, p. 65.
49. Ref. No. 22, p. 44.
50. Ref. No. 5. pp. 153-154.
51. Ref. No. 14, pp. 210-211.
52. Ref. No. 14, p. 211.
53. Ref. No. 35, pp. 77-78
54. Ref. No. 6, p. 319.
55. Ref. No. 12, p. 397.
56. Ref. No. 35, p. 138.
57. Ref. No. 8, p. 560.
58. Ref. No. 16, pp. 478-479.
59. Ref. No. 38, pp. 177-178.
60. Ref. No. 38, p. 286.
61. Ref. No. 26, pp. 58-59.
62. Ref. No. 2. p. 8.
63. Ref. No. 25, p. 82.
64. Ref. No. 26, p. 60.
65. Original letter in the possession of Christa von Kleist.
66. Ref. No. 26, p. 60.
67. Personal letter from Christa von Kleist to the author, 5-24-79.
68. Original death certificate in the possession of Christa von Kleist.

BIBLIOGRAPHY

1. Barker, A. J.: *Panzers at War.* New York: Charles Scribner's Sons, 1978.

2. Bidwell, Shelford: *Hitler's Generals and their Battles.* New York: Chartwell Books, 1976.

3. Buchner, Alex: *Der Bergkrieg im Kaukasus.* Friedberg: Podzun-Pallas-Verlag, 1977.

4. Carell, Paul: *Hitler Moves East.* New York: Ballantine Books, 1971.

5. Carell, Paul: *Scorched Earth.* New York: Ballantine Books, 1971.

6. Clark, Alan: *Barbarossa.* New York: William Morrow, 1965.

7. *Das Deutsche Heer 1939.* Bad Neuheim: Verlag Hans-Henning Podzun, 1953.

8. Davidson, Eugene: *The Trial of the Germans.* New York: Macmillan, 1966.

9. Fest, Joachim C.: *Hitler.* New York: Harcourt Brace Jovanovich, 1974.

10. Fraschka, Günter: *Mit Schwertern und Brillanten.* Rastatt: Erich Pabel Verlag, 1970.

11. *German Order of Battle 1944.* New York: Hippocrene Books, 1975.

12. Goebbels, Josef: *The Goebbels Diaries.* New York: Popular Library, 1948.

13. Graser, Gerhard: *Zwischen Kattegat und Kaukasus.* Tübingen: Kamaradenhilfswerk und Traditionsverband der ehemaligen 198.Infanterie-Division, 1961.

14. Hart, B. H. Liddel: *The German Generals Talk.* New York: William Morrow, 1948.

15. Haupt, W. and Wagener, C.: *Bildchronik der Heeresgruppe Süd.* Dorheim: Podzun-Verlag, 1969.

16. Höhne, Heinz: *The Order of the Death's Head.* New York: Coward-McCann, 1970.

17. Klietmann, Dr. K.-G.: *Die Waffen-SS — eine Dokumentation.* Osnabrück: Verlag "Der Freiwillige" G.m.b.H., 1963.

18. Macksey, Kenneth: *Guderian.* New York: Stein and Day, 1976.

19. Von Manstein, Erich: *Aus einem Soldatenleben.* Bonn: Athenäum-Verlag, 1958.

20. Von Manstein, Erich: *Lost Victories.* Chicago: Henry Regnery, 1958.

21. Majdalany, Fred: *The Fall of Fortress Europe.* New York: Modern Library Editions, 1968.

22. Von Mellenthin, F. W.: *German Generals of World War II.* Norman: University of Oklahoma Press, 1977.

23. Von Mellenthin, F. W.: *Panzer Battles.* Norman: University of Oklahoma Press, 1956.

24. *Mit dem K durch Frankreich (Erinnerungsbilder der Gruppe von Kleist).* Berlin: Verlag E. S. Mittler & Sohn, 1941.

25. Moll, Otto E.: *Die Deutschen Generalfeldmarschälle 1935-1945.* Rastatt: Erich Pabel Verlag, 1961.

26. Nehring, Walther K.: *Generalfeldmarschall Ewald v. Kleist,* in *Deutsches Soldatenjahrbuch 1974.* Munich: Schild-Verlag, 1974.

27. Nehring, Walther K.: *Die Geschichte der deutschen Panzerwaffe.* Stuttgart: Motorbuch Verlag, 1974.

28. Scheibert, Horst and Elfrath, Ulrich: *Panzer in Russland.* Dorheim: Podzun-Verlag, undated.

29. Schmitz, Günter: *Die 16.Panzer-Division 1938-1945.* Friedberg: Podzun-Pallas-Verlag, undated.

30. Von Seemen, Gerhard: *Die Ritterkreuzträger.* Friedberg: Podzun-Verlag, 1976.

31. Shirer, William L.: *The Rise and Fall of the Third Reich.* Greenwich: Fawcett, 1962.

32. *Soviet Panzers in Action.* Warren: Squadron/Signal Publications, 1973.

33. Taylor, Telford: *The March of Conquest.* New York: Simon and Schuster, 1958.

34. Taylor, Telford: *Sword and Swastika.* New York: Simon and Schuster, 1952.

35. Thorwald, Jürgen: *The Illusion.* New York: Harcourt Brace Jovanovich, 1975.

36. Toland, John: *Adolf Hitler.* New York: Doubleday, 1976.

37. Young, Peter (ed.): *Atlas of the Second World War.* New York: G. P. Putnam's Sons, 1974.

38. Ziemke, Earl F.: *Stalingrad to Berlin: The German Defeat in the East.* Washington: Office of the Chief of Military History, U.S. Army, 1968.

LANCER MILITARIA
Houston, Texas

Waddell Litho, Inc.

Houston, Texas 77098